D0983912

Leadership
Breakthrough

....

*Leadership Practices that Help Executives and
Their Organizations Achieve Breakthrough Growth*

KAREN LINDSEY

authorHOUSE®

AuthorHouse™
1663 Liberty Drive
Bloomington, IN 47403
www.authorhouse.com
Phone: 1-800-839-8640

© 2013 Karen Lindsey. All rights reserved.

No part of this book may be reproduced, stored in a retrieval system, or
transmitted by any means without the written permission of the author.

Published by AuthorHouse 09/23/13

ISBN: 978-1-4918-1495-6 (sc)
ISBN: 978-1-4918-1494-9 (hc)
ISBN: 978-1-4918-1493-2 (e)

Library of Congress Control Number: 2013916226

Any people depicted in stock imagery provided by Thinkstock are models,
and such images are being used for illustrative purposes only.
Certain stock imagery © Thinkstock.

This book is printed on acid-free paper.

Because of the dynamic nature of the Internet, any web addresses or links contained in
this book may have changed since publication and may no longer be valid. The views
expressed in this work are solely those of the author and do not necessarily reflect the
views of the publisher, and the publisher hereby disclaims any responsibility for them.

A special thank you to my husband, Michael, for his undying love and support; to my parents, Paul and Sue Kuhn, for inspiring me and being great role models; and to my dear friend, Linda, for her constant encouragement.

To my son, Aiden, the light of my life.

TABLE OF CONTENTS

INTRODUCTION

· ·

As executives climb the corporate ladder, and as business owners/entrepreneurs reach a point of consistent profitability, how do they keep the momentum going and continue to grow professionally? How do they continue to grow their organizations (people *and* the bottom line)? Most reach a plateau or a moderate growth rate that keeps them comfortable, at least for awhile. Eventually, their inability to keep up with the growth of their competitors or changes in their industry will lead to the premature cap of their career, loss of a job, or failure of their organization or company. They may not even realize they are hindering growth. The further up the ladder an executive climbs, the less time he or she spends on personal growth that can lead to organizational growth. For business owners, it is even more likely that personal growth is low on the list of priorities. Corporate executives have more resources at their disposal and are often required to participate in leadership growth programs in their organizations. When considering executive growth, what often gets overlooked or underestimated is the correlation between individual, professional growth and the growth of organizations.

In this book I discuss the key elements of leadership needed to reach the maximum growth potential of executives, business owners, and their organizations. While some of these key elements seem basic they continue to be the most neglected yet important leadership behaviors needed for achieving maximum growth and preventing an eventual decline in professional and organizational success. This book also covers concepts or ideas that will be new to some leaders who haven't been exposed to these leadership skills.

In my practice as an organizational and executive coach and leadership development consultant, I work with successful and identified "high-potential" executives who companies want to invest in for larger future leadership opportunities. I don't work with marginal or problem executives who companies are considering getting rid of. So the missing or underdeveloped leadership skills and behaviors I have identified for this book can be challenges, even for the most successful of executives. I continue to be amazed at the lack of focus on basic leadership qualities which hinders the growth of executives and their organizations and, if not addressed, can lead to the deterioration of careers, organizations, and companies. It's so easy to get wrapped up in the day-to-day fire drills and challenges when there are so many, and it's getting harder to find the time to focus on the long-term growth of individuals and companies. Unfortunately, this is a short-term reaction with potentially dangerous long-term implications.

The correlation between individual growth and organizational *success* is often forgotten, overlooked, or underestimated. I hear many executives and business owners express concern that focusing on their individual growth would appear self-serving. The growth areas I discuss in this book are specific to the individual but are directly related to organizational success and the bottom line.

If you are ready to restart your own professional growth while contributing to the growth of your organization or company, be prepared to challenge your current habits, develop or tune up some critical leadership skills, work smarter (not harder), and watch the positive impact on your whole organization.

CHAPTER 1

• •

Vision

A vision without a task is but a dream. A task without a vision is drudgery. A vision with a task is the hope of the world.

—Unknown

A clearly articulated, compelling, and propagated vision is more than just words on paper. There is a perception that *vision* has become one those trendy, overused leadership ideas or philosophies that every company has because it is expected to. Visions are often nebulous, abstract, and hard to quantify or measure; this makes them not only difficult to come up with and follow, but also subject to different interpretations by different people.

So, why is a vision important? A properly created vision helps guide and prioritize decision-making at all levels from the top of the organization to the individual contributors. Whether you're a manager of a three-person department, CEO of a company of ten thousand people, or owner of any sized company—a vision helps focus everyone on a common image of what their organization is working to achieve. Don't confuse *mission* with vision. I'm not talking about the mission statement of an entire enterprise that speaks to the purpose of an organization. I'm talking about a vision of the future for enterprises and organizations within an enterprise, from divisions down to small departments. A vision is a compelling statement (or two) that describes the desired future state of an organization. This also differs from *goals*, which are shorter term, very specific achievements to be made. There can be slightly different visions at each level of an organization as long as they are consistent and support a common vision. An example of a vision for a larger division might be to achieve a number two position in its market by the end of the year. An individual support department (finance, human resources, and so forth) may have a vision of creating demand for their services within the larger organization through proven added value, rather than having to fight to be included.

Before going any further, let me take a minute to define the terms that will be used to describe different levels of companies in this book. The term *organization* will be used as a generic term for any level of a company. Use it in a way that suits your situation. The term *enterprise* will be used for the largest and highest level of an organization. Examples include The Walt Disney Company, UTC, GE, and so on. The term *company* will be used to identify subsidiaries or independent companies of the larger enterprise. Examples would be The Walt Disney Studios, Pratt & Whitney, and GE Capital. *Divisions* are the organizations within a company typically determined by functional areas or product lines and comprised of numerous departments. Finally, *departments* are the lowest level of an organization comprised of individual contributors and typically designated according to function.

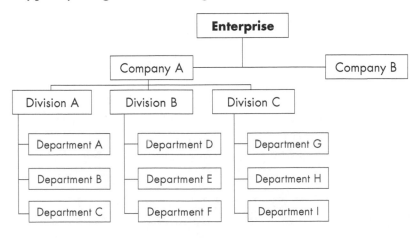

Without a clear vision there is often confusion about what an organization is trying to achieve other than a profit. Here's a great example. I coached the president of a software development company and conducted a *360 Assessment* on him. A 360 Assessment is a process whereby feedback is gathered from people all around the executive—supervisors, peers, direct reports, clients, and so on. It provides a 360-degree view of an executive's strengths and areas for growth and improvement. Some 360 Assessments are quantitative, using data gathered from questionnaires and ratings. Most of the 360 Assessments I conduct are interview style, so the feedback is gathered by interviewing participants; this provides a more qualitative and detailed assessment.

In this particular 360 Assessment during the interviews I asked what each employee thought the president's vision was for the future. I got different answers in each interview. Some thought it was purely financial—to hit some number of sales within two years by any means possible. Others thought it was to focus on standard, off-the-shelf solutions for customers. Still others thought it was to focus on custom solutions for customers. Clearly there was confusion about the direction of the organization. Decisions were being made every day based on which vision that particular leader or individual contributor thought the company was working toward. This is why clear, communicated visions are so important.

Before a vision is created, the proper homework should be done to ensure the vision is focused on the right messages. The right messages are those considered the most important—as determined internally (within the department or organization) and externally (with peer organizations, internal clients, and external customers). A great way to conduct this homework and research what the future state of your organization should look like is to conduct a 360 Assessment on the organization. Prepare a list of three to eight open-ended questions to ask individuals from within your organization (internal) and others that work with your organization (external). Open-ended questions start with *what*, *how*, or *why* and they elicit responses more in-depth than a simple *yes* or *no*. The use of open-ended questions can be a powerful way to promote creative and analytical thinking, which can uncover new solutions and opportunities. The power of using open-ended questions is further illustrated throughout this book. Questions that start with *why* should be used sparingly as they tend to focus on the past rather than opportunities and changes for the future.

The list of interviewees should start with all of the employees in your organization. Start here because you want your employees to understand what you're doing and why, while showing them that their opinion matters first. The questions might be slightly different for the internal employees and external employees. See exhibit 1-a for examples of questions for internal employees.

Exhibit 1-a: Questions for Internal Feedback

1. What does our organization do well?

2. What can our organization do better?

3. How well does our organization achieve goals and objectives?

4. How well does our organization work as a team? How can teamwork be improved?

5. What is the morale of our organization? How can it be improved?

6. In what other ways can our organization add value to the next larger entity (such as a division, company, or enterprise)?

Ask representatives of organizations that work with yours, up or down the process chain, supporting or being supported by your organization, or any other way that requires ongoing relationships. Do not avoid your biggest critics. They can provide the most insights into areas where your organization can improve. In fact, just asking their opinion in an open, honest, and non-defensive manner can help build relationships and teamwork. See exhibit 1-b for examples of questions for external employees.

Exhibit 1-b: Questions for External Feedback

1. What does the ____ organization do well?

2. What can the _____ organization improve upon?

3. How well does the ___ organization work with yours? How can the relationships be improved?

4. How effective is communication coming from the ___ organization? How can communication be improved?

5. What is the quality of the output received from the ___ organization? How can the quality be improved?

6. In what ways can the ____ organization add more value to the next larger entity (such as a division, company, or enterprise)?

Your list of open-ended questions should include at least a few very general questions that may help bring awareness to areas of focus that you haven't thought of before. Then a few more specific (but still open-ended questions) can be included if there are specific areas you want to gather feedback on.

Exhibit 1-c: Rules for Conducting 360 Assessments

1. If possible, conduct the assessments through face-to-face interviews. Interviews allow the interviewer to dig deeper when needed and adjust questions based on relationships and where the conversation goes if new or unexpected feedback comes up.

2. Most questions should be focused on the present or future to avoid too much dwelling on the past as questions about the past can quickly turn the conversation into an opportunity for just complaining. Questions about how things can be better in the future focus more on solutions.

3. All questions should be open-ended starting with primarily how and what.

4. Why questions should be kept to a minimum, as they tend to focus on the past.

5. Do not defend or object to any feedback provided. It will hinder the process and make it difficult to get further honest feedback. Ask more questions to clarify, and say thank you for the feedback.

6. Always include more than one source from each area associated with your organization—more than one peer group, more than one support group, more than one customer, etc.

7. Gather feedback from various levels—managers, executives, and individual contributors. It's not uncommon to have different opinions from different levels.

8. Don't let the feedback focus on any one individual in your organization. This is not the forum for that feedback.

9. If the interview starts to turn into an opportunity to just complain by the interviewee, redirect the conversation by asking future-oriented questions about what can be improved. upon or how. This helps focus on solutions rather than past problems.

There are some rules for conducting 360 Assessments to help ensure that the most honest and productive feedback is received. Exhibit 1-c provides a summary of rules for conducting 360s.

Visions can be short-term (one year) or long-term (five years), depending on the vision itself. A long-term vision needs to have shorter-term goals that can be reached each year. This will keep an organization focused on that vision, allow for small wins to keep motivation toward the vision, and ensure progress is being made. Anything over five years won't be effective for several reasons. It's hard for any of us to see beyond five years. The world is moving and changing so fast that the vision could become obsolete long before it's reached. Keeping a vision a priority becomes that much harder if it spans beyond five years.

A vision should be clear, concise, and described in as few words as possible. It should ideally be written in one paragraph and preferably in no more than two. The vision should be as specific as possible, incorporating numbers when it makes sense (for example, x% of increased sales, x% of reduced cost, x points in customer or employee satisfaction, and so on). But don't stop at the numbers. Add compelling language that describes what the department looks like in the end, such as "a place where people want to work" or "a department that is in demand." The more descriptive and inspiring the vision, the better. The vision also needs to be achievable —a stretch—but achievable.

The vision should be relevant. Consider the vision of the larger company and the goals being placed on your organization to make sure your vision is consistent. If you're stretching your organization beyond company expectations, it should be in a way that will be perceived as adding value to the organization or contributing to the bottom line. If it's not perceived as adding value it may appear to be a waste of effort or even a distraction from more important work.

The vision should be descriptive enough that you can identify when it has been achieved. This doesn't mean it has to be numbers driven and calculable, but it should include descriptions and words that would be used by others when describing the organization once the vision has been achieved. If your vision is more qualitative than quantitative, you may want to conduct a follow up 360 Assessment to determine the results. Exhibit 1-d provides questions to consider when creating a vision.

Exhibit 1-d: Consider These Questions When Creating a Vision
- What will have changed when the vision is reached?
- What specific goals will be achieved? (sales growth, cost reductions, customer satisfaction, employee satisfaction, etc.)
- What will the perception be from the outside of the organization?
- How well does it align with the goals of the larger company and those imposed on this organization?

Most organizations have a breadth of personalities that are motivated differently. A well-written vision should speak to all of them. Some people are motivated by competition, so using competitive language such as *being number one*, or beating a competitor in some way will inspire them. Some are motivated by numbers. For example, many salespeople are motivated by quotas because of the commissions they will earn. They may roll their eyes at the descriptive words in the vision. Others might be bored by numeric goals but motivated by inspiring words that describe the look and feel of success when it's achieved. Examples include being an organization others are trying to get into, or creating demand for your department. Consider the personalities of those involved and—hopefully, with their input—create a vision that speaks to them all while being in concert with the goals established by stakeholders (owners, management, corporate, and so forth. depending on the size of your organization). Often a vision statement will have numeric and descriptive terms. Exhibit 1-e provides examples of clear visions.

Exhibit 1-e: Examples of Visions

"We will rise to #2 in the market for banking software services by the end of 20xx."

"We will increase customer satisfaction scores by 25% in fiscal year 20xx by partnering with our customers to resolve their business issues."

"We will increase employee satisfaction scores to an average of 4.5 by year-end 20xx making this a happier and more fulfilling place to work."

"We will generate demand for our financial support services internally through teamwork, building relationships, and adding new value to our company by the end of 20xx."

"We will expand our services to include vendor management with 40% of our existing clients by the end of 20xx."

"We will focus our business going forward on custom software solutions and support generating 40% of revenues from that business by the end of 20xx."

"We will become a leaner and more productive organization by increasing revenue by 10% and reducing costs by 15% by the end of fiscal year 20xx."

"We will rebuild our reputation and employee morale by hitting our project budgets and milestones, and by providing designs with technical integrity by the end of 20xx."

Achieving buy-in is critical to the success of a vision. Buy-in needs to be obtained by those in the organization who will be responsible for reaching the vision (typically direct reports), as well as by stakeholders who need to agree on where efforts are being prioritized. The best way to achieve buy-in by those within the organization is to develop the vision with their participation. They will be more likely to own and work toward a vision that they helped create. This will also help promote teamwork. It's sad to watch and hear a leader make a grand statement about a new vision and see that those responsible for it in the organization are either surprised (because they hadn't heard about it yet) or rolling their eyes because they hadn't bought into it yet. That vision is doomed to fail.

Creating a vision gets you halfway there. As a leader, it is then your responsibility to make sure that vision is successful. The minute a vision gets forgotten, its leader loses some credibility. That leader becomes just another leader who is all talk and no action. He or she becomes much less effective because now his or her staff doesn't know which decisions will stick and which won't. The leader's future decisions will hold less weight and will not promote action because the staff will wonder if that new decision will just go away as well. If the vision changes, communicate that—formally and in a timely manner—but don't just let the vision fizzle out.

Once the vision has been written and bought into by those responsible for achieving it (as well as by the stakeholders), it's time to make that vision a reality. This doesn't happen overnight, and it requires diligent efforts to constantly move forward on that vision while managing day-to-day business.

Achieving the vision is similar to managing any large project and it can utilize basic project management principles with schedules, milestones, and budgets. Some organizations go so far as to give the vision project a pet name, catchy phrase, or slogan. That's a great way to give the vision a personality and an easy way to reference it. Another way to get the organization involved is to hold a contest to come up with the name or slogan.

How to Achieve a Vision

Now that the vision has been written, the first step in turning it into a reality is the hardest but most important for ensuring success—*planning*. Just like any project, achieving a vision requires planning. It's not enough to just say, "Now we have a vision; implement it." How?

The first step in the planning process is breaking the vision down into **actions**. What needs to happen for the vision to be achieved? What meetings need to occur? What verbal and/or written communication needs to be made? What research needs to be completed? What procedural changes need to occur? What behaviors need to change? Each component of the vision should have actions associated with it. In most cases, there will be many actions because, after all, this is a vision of the future state of your organization. Keep in mind, actions are just that—actions—that start with verbs. They have to be physical things that need to get done, not ideas or descriptions. This can be an exciting step because you'll start to see the possibilities of your vision become probabilities by identifying the actions required to get there. A vision alone without a plan can seem daunting because it's a description of the future and the *how* can seem overwhelming. When the vision is turned into actionable steps, the *how* becomes more definable and clear.

Exhibit 1-f is an example of a vision plan for the last vision in exhibit 1-e: "We will rebuild our reputation and employee morale by hitting our project budgets and milestones, and by providing designs with technical integrity." Each step may require further, more detailed action plans. Keep in mind that this vision would have been created with input and participation from the organization itself, so buy-in and any company approvals have already been established.

Exhibit 1-f: Example of Vision Plan for "We will rebuild our reputation and employee morale by hitting our project budgets and milestones, and by providing designs with technical integrity by the end of 20xx."

Action	Lead	Due Date
1. Schedule kickoff meeting with participants	John Smith	January 31, 20xx
2. Communicate vision plan to organization and company	John Smith	February 28, 20xx
3. Research project management software requirements and provide recommendations	Mike Smith	February 28, 20xx
4. Achieve approval for capital investment and expense allocation	John Smith/ Susan Field	March 15, 20xx
5. Implement new project management software	Mike Smith	April 15, 20xx
6. Determine and communicate design review procedures	Lisa Noonan	April 30, 20xx
7. Design and deliver project management training	Gus Johnson	May 31, 20xx

Exhibit 1-f: Example of Vision Plan for "We will rebuild our reputation and employee morale by hitting our project budgets and milestones, and by providing designs with technical integrity by the end of 20xx."

Action	Lead	Due Date
8. Monitor project budgets, schedules, and design review participation	John Smith/ Susan Field	Weekly
9. Design and produce new internal road show presentation	John Smith and Project Leads	June 30, 20xx
10. Present new and improved organization to the company	John Smith and Project Leads	July 31, 20xx
11. Celebrate	Everyone	July 31, 20xx

By the way, just like involving the organization in writing the vision can be a benefit, including the organization in creating the plan can have the same benefits—buy-in, new ideas on how to get the vision achieved, a sense of teamwork, and so forth. This will also help with the next step—<u>accountability</u>. Ideally, the entire organization should be held accountable to the vision in its entirety. Some actions (like behavioral changes) may be required by all, while others might involve select individuals. Whatever the case may be, each actionable step needs to have the responsible individuals identified.

Now that we have the *what* (vision), the *how* (actionable steps), and the *who* (accountable individuals), the piece that's missing is the *when*. Each actionable step needs to have a deadline or series of milestones attached to it. Again, these deadlines or milestones should be created with involvement by those being held accountable to help achieve buy-in as well as agreed upon, realistic dates. The planning step is now complete. Let implementation begin!

As achieving the vision gets underway, the next step—*checking progress*—becomes an ongoing activity. The best forums for ongoing progress updates is the weekly department or direct reports meetings. If you don't have a weekly meeting, please see chapter 8. There's an added benefit to discussing progress at these weekly meetings other than progress updates. It provides a constant, consistent reminder and reinforcement of the importance of the vision. There's no better way to keep the message going and incorporate it into day-to-day thinking and decision-making.

Goals, expectations, and even behavioral changes associated with the vision should be incorporated in the yearly performance objectives of everyone in the organization. This provides personal accountability for each individual in helping achieve the vision and, again, reinforces the importance of the vision. Building on the example used above for the vision and vision plan, examples of goals for individuals within this organization would be:

- Participate in the development of project budgets and milestones
- Meet or beat each project budget
- Meet or beat each project milestone
- Attend all design review meetings
- Build relationships with other design departments

Everyone in the organization must be held accountable for his or her responsibilities in achieving the vision. The supporters of the vision should be encouraged and acknowledged. Efforts should be made to transform the skeptics of the vision to supporters. The blockers or skeptics who can't be transformed need to be removed. Blockers can make it incredibly difficult—and in some cases impossible—for visions to be achieved, as they may sabotage any efforts and hurt the teamwork and morale needed to be successful.

Recognition and Rewards

The final step to achieving the vision is **recognition and rewards**. There's a reason I listed recognition before rewards—contrary to the popular phrase *rewards and recognition*. Recognition will come before rewards and will continue on an ongoing basis, while rewards are typically given toward the end. Find every opportunity to recognize positive movement toward the vision by acknowledging the work and accomplishments and by thanking those responsible. Recognizing individuals' contributions publicly within the organization will reinforce the importance of the vision, demonstrate that you are watching, and motivate others to contribute. Recognize every effort made toward the vision. The positive reinforcement will help motivate and, yet again, reinforce the importance of the vision. It might also create some peer pressure and healthy competition around achieving the vision.

On the flip side of positive recognition, attention can also be given to the efforts that do not support the vision and used as examples of what *not* to do. This is a great way to reinforce the vision and demonstrate how efforts contrary to the vision are not acceptable. This should be done carefully, with tact, and with proper leadership etiquette focusing on the behaviors and not on the person.

At the end, when the vision has been achieved, it's time to celebrate! Make a big deal about this achievement. Have a celebratory luncheon or happy hour. Consider buying a personalized commemorative gift for everyone in the organization—T-shirts, watches, paperweights, and so forth. If possible, find a way to communicate the success throughout the company to bring recognition and visibility to your organization.

Now it's time to create another vision to take your organization to the next level.

Summary

Having a vision helps an <u>executive</u> grow by focusing on the potential future state of his or her organization. It provides an opportunity to create a strategic direction and to practice leadership skills driving the organization to a common goal and achieving it.

Visions help <u>organizations</u> grow by providing thought, leadership, and focus toward a potential future state that is bought into, supported, and achieved by everyone in the organization. It ensures that decisions are being made every day at every level to support the strategic direction of the organization.

CHAPTER 2:

∙ ∙

Time & Energy Management, Allocation & Focus

Time is the scarcest resource and unless it is managed nothing else can be managed.

—*Peter Drucker*

While time management may seem like a fairly tactical topic, it continues to be a significant challenge for executives. As an executive coach, I see this issue come up with 90 percent of my clients. Everyone feels overwhelmed by all that needs to be done. In this fast-paced world of infinite information that's immediately available through many digital media, and with technology advancing at an exponentially growing rate, it's impossible to keep up with everything we can add to our list. Keep in mind, it's not just about time management; it's about *energy* management, too. How and where we put our energy is just as important as where we devote our time. If we're sitting in a meeting (spending time) but distracted about something else (spending energy), we're giving *neither* the proper attention; this is ineffective and draining. Time (and energy) management becomes critical to ensuring that the right things are being focused on individually and as an organization. Ineffective time management can lead to significant problems including:

- Late delivery on milestones
- Things falling through the cracks
- Missed opportunities that may be caught by competitors
- Considerable inefficiencies
- Lack of attention to strategy, leadership, and talent development
- Employee burnout and poor morale

The behaviors that lead to poor time management and focus include:

- Allowing distractions from phone calls, emails, and unproductive or unimportant fire drills
- Delegating ineffectively
- Losing accountability
- Prioritizing poorly
- Using ineffective time management tools and processes
- Attending too many ineffective and inefficient meetings

I have seen executives get buried and fail because they couldn't manage their time, efforts, projects, and staff well. I continue to be amazed at the lack of prioritization on the right efforts and wasted time on the wrong ones. Every minute of every day we make choices on how we spend our time. Our choices may not be conscious or fire drills can lead us down paths of tasks without our realizing how we're spending our time. We mindlessly follow these paths, regardless of their relative importance and effectiveness. This can lead to inefficiencies and wasted efforts. If we take the time to make sure that we're focused on the right activities every minute of every day, we will maximize our efficiencies, effectiveness, and productivity. An effective time management process can help us do that.

The first step to creating an effective time management process is to

organize your environment. *How does this help your time management?* you may ask. Chances are if you have a disorganized office, your environment is contributing to your lack of efficiency. You may have hidden tasks all over your desk—things that have fallen through the cracks, incomplete projects, or just clutter that's in the way. You may be spending too much time looking for important notes, papers, or files. There may be too many items on your desk that can lead to distractions when you should be focusing your time elsewhere.

Another way a disorganized office can impact your effectiveness is the psychological toll it takes just looking at it. How many times have you looked at the piles and messiness and exhaled in frustration, exhaustion, or the feeling of being overwhelmed?

Organizing your office will help you create an effective means of managing the paperwork, projects, tasks, and clutter, and will help you focus your energy where it needs to be. Spend the time creating a filing system that works for you, throwing away papers you don't need, and gathering those that require action or follow up.

Start with at least four piles (or more if needed): one for documents to file and keep, one for the "circular file" (garbage or recycling), one for items to delegate, and one for items that require action or follow-up on your part.

If you're anything like me, with a tendency to hoard, deciding what to throw away can be challenging and can even create some anxiety. After all, what if I need that piece of paper, old report, or last month's article in the future? The good news is that in today's digital world, most information can be fairly easily accessed if or when needed. In fact, very few pieces of paper need to be stored anymore. Exceptions would be information you need quick access to, paperwork you're currently working on, or legal documents with signatures that need to be kept. Old articles can be found on the Internet. Old reports are saved or archived digitally if not by you then by the originator of the report; they can therefore be obtained again if needed. For each piece of paper, report, article, or any other paperwork on your desk that you don't currently need, ask yourself if you can obtain the information again if you need it. If the answer is *yes*, throw it away. Hopefully the "circular file" pile will be the larger of the piles you're creating. It will feel so good to file this pile away!

Next, create an effective filing system *that works for you*. Think about how you work and how you categorize things in your mind—and file accordingly. What will work better for you—filing chronologically? By client? By project? Make your files and file away! If you have an assistant, engage him or her in the process. Ask for help. If not, consider enlisting an intern or even paying for a temp to help. Keep in mind that you are not engaging in just a cleanup. The intent is to create a filing system that will work for you going forward to keep yourself organized. By enlisting your assistant, he or she will be better able to support you with filing and finding needed documents.

Delegate the items in your delegation pile. Keep track of those you need to follow up on. The next chapter will cover more on effective delegation.

At this point, you may feel some sense of accomplishment and hope about getting organized and more efficient. You may also be feeling a bit overwhelmed at all the things you found that need action or follow up—which brings us to the final pile. You'll be adding these items into your new time management system. Don't get discouraged yet. We're just getting started. You'll be creating a plan to address these items.

How do you keep your environment organized going forward? One method that works successfully for many is to clean your desk/office (including your inbox) at the end of every day before leaving work. Some people do the same thing once a week, typically on Fridays. By doing so, you will be and feel more organized, stay on top of work that needs to be done or delegated, and prevent anything from falling through the cracks.

Before we get into your new time management system, we need to **find the tool** that's right for you. An effective time management system includes a calendar and task management component. The key is finding the tool or tools that fit with your personality and way of thinking. I believe the reason so many people try time management systems but don't stick with them is that the tool they're trying to use doesn't "fit" them, or there's something about it they just don't like but haven't identified. There are many time management tools on the market—paper day-timers, PDAs, computer software, apps, online websites, and so forth. There are also those simpler, self-created systems like keeping the list in your head, the old but often-used gigantic paper list of all lists, or sticky-notes. I don't recommend the latter three.

The time management tool must have several elements to be effective. See exhibit 2-a.

Exhibit 2-a: Requirements for Effective Time Management

1. A calendar with daily, weekly, and monthly views

2. A task management component

3. The ability to plan tasks daily in the short-term (one week maximum) and document tasks for the future

4. Portability—must be able to carry it with you

An effective time management system allows you to merge the management of time and tasks. You will be able to prioritize tasks and fit them into your calendar effectively. First you need a calendar component with daily, weekly, and monthly views. The daily view allows you to manage your daily tasks and meetings, return phone calls you need to make, emails you need to write, and any other follow-ups for the day. The weekly view allows you to look ahead to manage meetings and deadlines for the week, tasks that have to be done this week but not today, and today's tasks that need to be moved. The monthly view allows you to add or move tasks not required for the week further out without losing sight of them and to manage events, meetings, and any other significant dates for the month—even birthdays and other special occasions. The task component is nothing more than space in your tool for each view (daily, monthly) for writing tasks, phone calls, follow-ups, and anything else that needs to get done.

Find a tool that will work for you. The questions in exhibit 2-b might help. Then research the tools that are available. Search the web. Ask others who are particularly organized what they use. Go to a bookstore or electronics department. Keep in mind that the tool you select does not have to dictate your process. Too many people abandon the tools they try because a particular function or component of the tool (or implied process) doesn't resonate with them. Create the process that works for you and find a tool that supports it. For example, my chosen tool is FranklinCovey's day planner. I like many of its features but they don't all work for me. I've added some features and uses of my own, and I don't use some of the features that come with it. I have my own tailored system that works for me, but I use the FranklinCovey planner as my primary tool. When creating your process, think about how you like to work or plan. Do you start with a calendar and then think about tasks? Or do you start with tasks and then work in your calendar? When you visualize your calendar or schedule, what does it look like? Are the days listed (in your mind) top to bottom or across horizontally? Think about a project or time in your life when you were the most organized. What made you so organized then? What tools or process did you use? If at this point you're still struggling with finding a tool, continue reading through the time management steps and you'll have a better idea at the end of what you want your tool to look like.

Exhibit 2-b: Ask Yourself These Questions When Looking for a Time Management Tool

Do I prefer writing or typing?

How much time do I spend at my desk versus on the road?

Do I want to use an electronic tool such as a handheld device?

Do I want access to my task list on my computer and handheld device?

How large or small does it need to be for me to carry it and use it?

Do others (such as an assistant) need access to it?

Time Management Process

The first step in creating your time management process is to **take a written inventory** of everything on your "list" (written and in your head) of things that need to be done—every project, phone call, task, follow-up, or reminder. Write it *all* down on one list. Write down anything and everything that's in your head that needs to be done as well as any goals you want to reach. We want to capture everything that takes mental energy either as reminders of what needs to get done or goals that are on your mind. This includes small tasks like picking up a birthday card for a friend and larger projects like researching a new insurance policy. At this point many of you have sighed and now have a pit in your stomach from feeling overwhelmed at the thought of how big that list will get or how long it will take to write everything down—let alone achieve them. Your list may get really big with well over a hundred items, but stick with me. The whole point is managing all of these things. By not writing them down they don't go away, so let's proactively manage them. If you can, put them in a spreadsheet program such as Excel, which will make sorting easier later.

One of the biggest sources of stress for many of us is the number of things on our minds that we are trying to remember to do. We think of these things at odd times in meetings, at dinner, when we're supposed to be listening to someone talk, or in the middle of the night remembering little things we forgot or want to remember to do. An effective time (and energy) management process will help you be so organized you won't have to rely on memory. Everything will be written down and organized so you can address each individual item when the time is right. Think of all the brain cells you can free up!

Next, break down the larger projects into steps or tasks. We need to break down each item into an *action* (with a verb) versus an idea or project. For example, *strategic plan* is a project. The steps might be to set up a kickoff meeting, review last year's plan, establish a timeline, and so on. Those are action items. Another example might be *health insurance*, a project. The steps might be to find the previous policy, prepare a list for quotes, call for quotes, research companies, call an agent, and so forth.

Should you include personal items? That's up to you. If you don't do it now, chances are you will incorporate them into your system later. If you want to manage them but don't want to co-mingle with business items, keep a separate list but write it in the same place for each day, week, or month so you can schedule them into your "free" or non-working time.

Now that you have everything on your list, let's break it down. While we have a tendency to think that everything needs to be done *now* and we put pressure on ourselves thinking that, the reality is everything *can't* be done now. So, let's accept that and make sure the right things are done at the right time. We're talking about prioritizing. The keys to prioritizing are being *realistic* and challenging yourself. We have a tendency to overestimate how *long* something (a task or step versus a large project) will actually take, how *urgent* something is, or how important it is that *we* do it all. Add three columns next to your list. The first added column is *delegation*, the second is *duration* and the third is *date*. Now ask yourself these questions for each item and put your responses in the appropriate columns. *Remember, be realistic and challenge yourself to be honest.*

1. Who else can or should do this? (See delegation for more information.)
2. How long will this task take?
3. When does it need be done or started? (If it's a project with a deadline, include the date you need to get started with the first task.)

Now you should have a complete list of everything you need to do and the data needed to sort it. If you've put your list in Excel, this will be easier. Start by sorting the data by date. Combine those items that are for next year or future years into one list and put that list in the back of your time management tool (calendar or daytimer if in written form) or in an easy-to-find file on your PDA or computer. The idea is to keep this list available to add to or adjust when needed but not have it be a constant thought or bother now when you don't need it. We want to file these future goals or tasks so we don't lose sight of them, but also keep them from taking mental energy *now*. In your mind it's like thinking *I know I want to do these in the future and I've done what I can today to prepare for that by documenting it and putting it away to be scheduled later. I don't have to think about it until I need to.* While the mind may or may not do a great job remembering things, the mind does not know *when* to remember them—hence, the middle-of-the-night reminders. By writing something down (or typing it), you free your mind from having to remember it. This might not happen right away. But over time as you get used to your time management process, you will begin to trust it, and your mind will learn to let go. It's similar to writing something down when you think of it at 2:00 a.m. so you can get back to sleep.

Now do the same thing for future quarters. Combine a list for the next three quarters and put them in your calendar on the first day of the respective quarter. Those lists will be addressed when the time is right. For now, let them go—mentally knowing that they are where they need to be, documented to be addressed when appropriate. This is important for managing our energy.

Narrowing the list down even further, break apart the remaining items (which should be the current quarter's) into the three months of the quarter (or however many months there are left of the current quarter). Put the lists for the future months in your calendar at the first day of the month. It needs to be easily found and accessed so you can add to it and make changes as they occur.

Now we can focus on the current month, week, and day. First, make sure all of your meetings and appointments are scheduled in your calendar for the month. By the way, this is a great time to be thoughtful about which meetings you attend. Which meetings do you have to go to and why? Which meetings can you delegate? Loading all of your essential meetings first will not only help you keep your appointments, but also will help you see how much time you have available to *do* the things on your list. Load the remaining tasks into your calendar on the dates they need to be done or started. As you do this, you may see that some days have too many items that can't possibly get done in that day. Reference the durations for each item that you captured in your original list. You have the opportunity to proactively deal with time conflicts now versus waiting until that day when you get panicked and miss deadlines or have to cancel plans. Move items ahead or behind as appropriate to make your schedule work. I can hear some of you now saying, "But all of these things *have* to get done that day." I hear that all the time. You may feel that way but in reality that may not be possible. You can only effectively do one thing at a time. Recognize that now and prepare for it by planning ahead.

Now you should be able to look at the week and see how each day looks—what meetings you have and what tasks need to be done. You may want to schedule your tasks on your calendar like a meeting by blocking the time. Some people like doing this and some don't. You can also keep a prioritized task list for each day with your calendar to reference and help keep you focused between meetings. Again, the idea is to make your time management process fit you so you're more likely to stick with it and use it. The important thing is to prioritize and do the right things at the right time.

Let's look at today in more detail and prioritize what needs to be done. This is an exercise you will be doing at the start of every day. Prioritize the items that need to be done based on urgency and importance. Write (or type) numbers (1, 2, 3 ...) or letters (A, B, C ...) next to each item based on priorities. Then follow that plan throughout the day. As items get completed, put a check mark or any symbol you prefer to designate that the item has been completed. As items get started but will continue tomorrow or another day in the future, put another designated symbol next to them to show that they are in progress, and immediately schedule the next step or follow up so it doesn't get forgotten. I use a dot (from the FranklinCovey system), but feel free to create your own. The items that will not get started today as originally planned need to be moved forward to tomorrow or another day, as appropriately prioritized. Designate a symbol for those items, and right after you put that symbol next to those items immediately write those items again on the future dates that you plan to do them. This is important. If you don't plan for them right away, you risk assigning the wrong priorities, or forgetting them entirely letting those items fall through the cracks. Those items that can be delegated but that you need to follow up on will have their own designated symbol. Decide what you want to use for that. As you mark that symbol next to the appropriate items, plan for when you're going to follow up by writing those tasks on the days you want to follow up. Now you'll know to do that when the time is right and they won't be forgotten. Finally, designate a symbol for cancelled or deleted items. Use this symbol for items you no longer have to address either now or in the future. Examples of symbols are in exhibit 2-c.

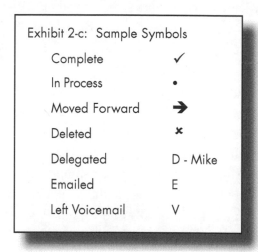

Exhibit 2-c: Sample Symbols	
Complete	✓
In Process	•
Moved Forward	→
Deleted	✗
Delegated	D - Mike
Emailed	E
Left Voicemail	V

The same process applies to phone calls, emails, and texts. When you've finished a phone call, email, or text use your designated symbol for completed items. If you leave a message for someone or need to follow up with another phone call, use your designated symbol for continuing items and write down the follow up on the appropriate future day.

At the end of each day, each item should have a symbol next to it; those items that are continuing or need to be followed up on have been planned accordingly. I have two rules that really help me stay current and prevent things from falling through the cracks. In my day planner, any time I write a symbol for an item that requires rescheduling, further attention, or follow up, I must reschedule immediately or schedule a follow up *before* I can write that symbol next to that item. I also do not let myself move the page finder to the next day until all items for today have symbols by them and have been dealt with accordingly. If you stick to this process each day, you will never have to look backwards in your calendar to figure out what needs to be done now or in the future. You can just keep focusing on today, look ahead, and never look back!

As mentioned before, the first reason many people abandon time management tools and processes is the frustration from trying to use tools or processes that don't fit them. The second reason people abandon the process is frustration from dealing with the many changes that constantly happen to schedules, tasks, and priorities. I see so many people throw up their hands in frustration asking, "What's the point if everything is just going to change anyway?" But this is exactly the point. The more organized we are with our schedules and priorities, the easier it will be to manage the changes. We can't look at change— whether it's a large macro change or a smaller change in schedule— as a problem and resist it. That will only make it harder to adjust to; meanwhile, the change still happens. Take control of change by proactively adjusting to it and planning around it. There will be days when every symbol seen on that day is the designated symbol for things that are not completed and need to be moved to another day. Accept that. It will happen. What's more important is how you *deal* with it. Manage change; don't let change manage *you*. Stay in control. Some feel like it's a failure if nothing on the list for the day is accomplished. Change that mindset. Failure is letting things go and not managing change appropriately so things fall through the cracks, focus gets lost, and we feel overwhelmed again.

Fit any changes or fire drills into your schedule, even if they're immediate, and plan accordingly. When fire drills occur and you start to panic or get stressed about how it's all going to get done, take a minute to look at your schedule, make sure you've delegated everything you can delegate, move things around and forward in your schedule (meetings and tasks), then focus on the issue at hand. You will manage your time better, be and stay organized, and adjust more easily to fire drills. You will also feel more in control, more focused, and more confident—but much less stressed.

Load in all scheduling changes and additions as soon as you know about them. Write (or type) them down *immediately*. That's why you should keep your time management tool with you at all times. This will help you manage the changes or additions, prevent them from being forgotten, and allow you to free up your mind from having to remember them. Get them down, schedule them, and move on.

Now you have a plan to get and stay organized. The next step is maintaining focus and building discipline around prioritizing your efforts. It's one thing to prioritize in writing; it's another to adhere to that prioritization. It's so easy to get distracted by over-exaggerated fire drills, things that are more fun to do, things that fall into your comfort zone, or just anything that can be an excuse from doing that awful task you are procrastinating doing.

Remember, each moment of each day you decide consciously or unconsciously how you're spending that time. Keep it conscious. Make a decision on what you should and will do with each moment. Ask yourself, "Is this what I should be doing right now?" and challenge yourself to keep the reasons legitimate. I'm sure you can come up with many reasons to do what you want in that moment. Make sure the reason is real. When new things come up, don't let yourself get distracted by them just because they are new. Schedule and prioritize them accordingly. Write them down and get back to what you should be doing.

I recommend to my clients that they turn off whatever noise their handheld device or computer makes when a new email, text, or IM comes in. According to *The New York Times* bestseller *The Power of Habit* by Charles Duhigg, checking emails and texts can actually become almost an addiction—something we crave. The cue that drives this addiction is often the sound or vibration the device or computer makes. We hear or feel that cue and automatically reach for the device or computer to satisfy our craving. If we remove those cues, we are less likely to be distracted by these cravings. Check your emails, texts, IMs and voicemails when it's convenient and time effective for you. Plan specific times each day that you will check them. Do not let them be distractions.

The single most common frustration I consistently hear about is how much time it takes reading, responding to, and managing emails. In fact, for many it's a significant source of stress. There are many reasons for that. Many people receive more emails than they can manage in a day. Combing through that volume of emails to find the important ones is very inefficient. There's also a perceived urgency due to the speed of communication and noise our handheld devices or computer makes when we receive them. Then there's the addiction mentioned earlier. The key to managing our email is to control it and not be controlled *by* it.

There are things we can do to more effectively control our email inboxes. Some require us to change some habits and control our fear that we may miss something important if we get fewer emails. Keep in mind that chances are very high that anything important will be brought to your attention another way if not by email. Here are some tips for managing your inbox and the distractions it creates:

- Unsubscribe to any email lists you don't need to be on.
- *Immediately* unsubscribe to any new ones you don't need.
- Ask to be taken off of distribution lists for emails you don't read.
- Only read emails for which you are included in the *To* list— and not those you are only *cc'd* on.
- Ask those you regularly communicate with not to *cc* you on emails and to bring important information to your attention another way.
- Be honest with yourself about which emails you're really going to read later. If you have to think about whether or not you will, you probably won't get to it.
- Forward (delegate) emails that can and should be addressed or read by others.
- If you have a capable and knowledgeable assistant, have him or her screen your emails for you.
- Don't respond to emails you are only *cc'd* on unless it's to correct or add important information.
- Don't respond to emails unless you're providing new information—not just comments (since this just creates more emails for everyone).

- Respond to emails requiring a response within 24 – 48 hours, even if it's just to say you'll have to get back to the recipient at a later time.
- Create folders to sort and save important emails (so they don't clutter your inbox).
- Consider taking the topic "offline" after three responses from you and/or others. It probably requires a phone or in-person discussion.
- Schedule time weekly or monthly to clear out your inbox if it gets too cluttered.

Many people who complain about the volume of emails received are afraid to do anything about it out of fear of being kept out of the loop or of missing something. Yet it's possible to miss something anyway as they quickly try to sift through all of them. Remember, if there's something important you need to know, it will be brought to your attention if not in the *To* line than via phone or in person. I strongly encourage leaders to build a culture in which important discussions do not happen over email (for many reasons discussed in chapter 7). Leaders can also be role models in their organizations for the best way to handle and use email. Some leaders create rules in their organizations for how emails are to be used. This can be an effective way to streamline that form of communication so it's used efficiently and doesn't become a time waster and distraction for everyone.

When you get distracted (by emails or anything else) and lose or change focus from one task to another, it can take up to twenty minutes to reengage in the original task. Think about how many distractions you get in a day and how much time is wasted reengaging. Think about how much more productive you can be by managing those distractions and staying focused.

Throughout the day, I encourage you to refer back to your schedule and priorities for the day to help you stay focused and make adjustments as necessary. One of my clients refers to his time management tool as his anchor. When he starts to feel out of control or without focus, he refers back to his schedule and anchors himself and his focus where it needs to be. If you start to feel anxiety because something is taking longer than expected or you can't seem to get to something and it's bothering you, refer back to your schedule and move things around—or re-prioritize as necessary to help you feel in control and focused again.

Now that you see how a time management process can work, review the guidelines earlier in the chapter for choosing a time management tool; find the tool that's best for you or evaluate the one you're currently using. You may have to try several different formats or types of time management tools to find the one that works for you. If you start to feel a sense of dread every time you look at your tool, you've picked the wrong one. Think about why you don't like it and change it, or find a tool that provides what you're looking for. When you have found or created the tool that works for you and successfully manage your process, you won't dread using it. It will help you and you will rely on it to help you. Give yourself time to adjust to it and make changes to your liking, and it will become your most valuable tool. I'm able to keep my stress under control and maintain focus on my priorities knowing I have everything written down and planned for—to be addressed when appropriate. Exhibit 2-d provides a summary of the steps to start your time management system.

Exhibit 2-d: Steps to Start Time Management System

1. Organize your environment.

2. Write inventory of all to-do's.

3. Break down larger projects into actions.

4. Determine delegation opportunities, durations, and due dates (or start dates) for each item.

5. Separate list by year, current year's quarters, current month, and this week.

6. Plan meetings, tasks, etc. by day for the current week.

7. Prioritize tasks for today

The final point on time (and energy) management is getting comfortable saying *no* when you can't take on more and learning to ask for help when you have too much. We have a tendency to feel pressure—which is often self-inflicted—to say *yes* to everything we're asked to do, whether it's taking on someone else's work, volunteering at our children's school, volunteering at church, or helping friends or family with chores or errands. Get comfortable saying *no* when you need to. The key to saying *no* is not feeling like we have to explain why. We get caught up in our excuses and whether or not we think the other person will think they're legitimate. Just say: "I'm sorry, I would love to help you with *x* but I just can't right now." If they ask why, repeat: "I just can't fit it in right now." There might be a moment of uncomfortable silence as the other person tries to absorb what they've heard. It may take them a minute to accept the fact that you've taken away their power to argue with you—as you've not provided information they can argue with.

Don't be afraid to ask for help. Delegate when you can to your staff or family. Try to resist making assumptions about others' time availability or ability to take on more, and ask them. More often than not, when I challenge clients to ask others for help, my clients' immediate response is "They [others] don't have time." This assumption is made without even asking. When I challenge them to at least *ask*, more often than not the others can and do help. Others may not be as busy as you are or may have lower priorities and can fit your needs in. Most can take on more and are willing to. Give them the opportunity to help. The worst that can happen is that they will say *no*. Delegation will be addressed in more detail in the next chapter.

While learning to say *no* can be an effective way to manage your time and stick to priorities, don't abuse it. There are instances when saying *no* can hurt your growth and the growth of your organization. For example, saying *no* to a customer because you don't have time would not look good. Saying *no* to your boss is not recommended unless you have exhausted all possible ways of doing what has been asked. Even then I would think again and look harder for options. Bosses don't want to hear that something can't be done. This is particularly true the higher you are in the organization—where decisions, resources, and processes are under your control. You were hired and will be expected to find solutions and not present excuses.

The CEO of a billion dollar manufacturing and distribution organization explained to me that one of his biggest frustrations with those in his executive staff was their reluctance to evaluate and pursue new ideas because they didn't have time. These new ideas included acquisition opportunities, new product line opportunities, and new technology opportunities, all of which have the potential to help the organization (and executives) grow. In fact, *not* evaluating and pursuing such opportunities is a great example of how executives can hinder their own growth or the growth of their organizations and potentially hurt their organizations' ability to compete in the future.

It is not uncommon for executives to be reluctant to pursue new opportunities for fear of failure or their lack of ability (or desire) to take on more. In essence, these executives could be constraining their organization to the level they are comfortable managing. This is yet another example of how executives can hurt their growth and that of their organizations. Don't be one of those executives. Use your time management skills and help coach your organization in time management to help everyone—and the organization—grow.

Exhibit 2-e provides a summary of the steps to create an effective time management process.

Exhibit 2-e: Steps to an Effective Time Management Process

1. Organize Your Environment

2. Find Your Tool

3. Take Inventory

4. Delegate and Follow Up

5. Develop Your Plan

6. Proactively Ensure Success

7. Manage Changes

8. Manage Distractions

Exhibit 2-f offers the keys to keeping your time management process going forward. Follow these steps consistently and you are guaranteed to be a master of your time. If you fall behind, don't give up. Get caught up and keep going!

Exhibit 2-f: Keys to Lasting Time Management Success

1. Write everything down in one place (calendar and tasks).

2. Carry it with you.

3. Plan ahead every day and check in constantly.

4. Move forward and never look back.

5. Accept and manage change.

6. Ask yourself: Who else can and should do this?

7. Constantly ask yourself: Is this what I should be doing right now?

8. Learn to say no when appropriate.

So, how does effective time management impact the organization? If each executive—and each employee for that matter—worked more effectively and efficiently, think about the exponential impact on the organization. There would be less time spent on activities that provide little or no value. Each employee would be focusing their time and energy on the appropriate tasks at the appropriate time, while managing and even limiting fire drills. Delegation would be more effective as each level focuses on the tasks and issues appropriate for that level. More time would be available for the more important longer-term strategic decisions and projects.

As illustrated in exhibit 2-g, tasks or projects fall into one of four categories depending on their urgency and importance. Those items that are low in urgency and low in importance should be minimized. Items that are high in urgency and high in importance require immediate attention and the rescheduling of everything else. Those that are high in importance but low on urgency tend to be the important longer-term concerns that often don't get enough attention due to the lack of urgency. These items should be proactively planned for. Meanwhile, those that have an illusion of urgency because something triggers those tasks and gets our attention—emails, phone calls, and unexpected visitors—but may not be important often get immediate attention. Those items should be managed appropriately and given the proper priority to prevent them from being distractions.

Exhibit 2-g: Allocating Time	

	High	
	emails phone calls drop-by visitors	work stoppages emergencies deadlines
Urgency	mail wasteful meetings busy work	long-term planning reading about industry/marketplace researching competitors technical growth leadership development/ training
	Low	

Low	Importance	High

Summary

Efficient and effective time management helps <u>executives</u> grow by ensuring they focus on the right things at the right time. Projects, issues, and decisions will be given the appropriate time, energy, and priority. The executives can maximize their own productivity and increase performance. Confidence is also gained by feeling in control with the ability to manage fire drills as they occur—without foregoing the appropriate attention to the day-to-day business and important longer-term issues.

Successful time management of executives helps a <u>company</u> grow by maximizing the value of the executives and their teams and ensuring that time, energy, and priorities are allocated effectively. Projects and issues are less likely to fall through the cracks, and fire drills can be more easily managed. The company will be able to work more proactively and less reactively, and it will have time to devote to longer-term strategic opportunities.

CHAPTER 3:

●●●

Delegation

The best executive is the one who has sense enough to pick good men to do what he wants done, and self-restraint enough to keep from meddling with them while they do it.

—*Theodore Roosevelt*

Delegation is one of the more common skills executives are deficient in and yet it is key to leading and working effectively. There are many reasons to delegate effectively and many benefits to doing so. Effective delegation ensures the appropriate levels of an organization are working on the appropriate levels of work. This is determined based on the training, education, experience, skills, and talents of the individuals matched with the level of difficulty of the tasks or projects, access to needed information and resources, and degree of risk. Executives delegate to focus their time and efforts on higher-level strategic issues. Each level of an organization should be working on the appropriate level of work that should also include some stretch assignments that offer growth at each level.

The benefits of effective delegation are not just the time savings to you, but also the value the company receives from you and your organization. Delegation and sharing of the workload also offer growth opportunities for you, your staff, and the whole organization as each level continues to be challenged.

The more you delegate, the more time you have to contribute to your company on a more strategic level. Your company will receive better value from you because they won't be paying you for work that can be done by less expensive talent, and they will reap the benefits of your focus on the future. The higher up an individual climbs, the more time he or she should spend on future planning, strategic issues, and new opportunities for the company.

Effective delegation is something that should be encouraged at all levels, not just at the executive levels. Executives should be training and monitoring their organizations to ensure everyone is working at the appropriate level. This will allow the company to receive the value each position should be providing.

Delegating to your staff not only improves your efficiency, it also gives your staff the opportunity to grow and contribute at a higher level. Most employees would jump at the chance to take on higher-level work. It provides them with growth opportunities, the development of new skills, and potentially more visibility. Meanwhile, you get the benefit of having a more skilled staff, which could lead to more delegation opportunities and a chance to elevate your focus to an even higher level. You may also be preparing a possible future successor.

While coaching one of my clients, the general manager of a business unit for one of the largest media companies, we were focusing on her time management challenges to help her find time for the higher-level strategic issues her organization was facing. As we reviewed everything on her list of things to do, I realized she was doing the entire Five-Year-Plan for her business unit *herself* rather than delegating at least portions of it. Not only was this an inefficient use of her time, but also it was a missed opportunity for her staff. This was a great growth opportunity for her team to be included in the process and learn from it. She was encouraged to set the direction and theme of the plan, identify responsibilities and deadlines for each direct report, identify the person pulling all the pieces together, and monitor the progress along the way. This allowed her to free up some valuable time and gave her direct reports new opportunities and visibility.

I have had many clients resist delegating for fear of overwhelming their staff with too much to do. Yet every time I push them to try it, it is received with success and enthusiasm. There is a tendency to assume our staff can't take on more yet, more often than not, not only are they able to but also they are willing to. By delegating to them, you are helping them learn to delegate as well. They may be taking on more junior-level work than they should be. This is common. Whenever there is an opportunity to delegate, ask your staff to take it on. Don't be afraid to ask for extra effort, but be respectful of their personal lives. If they can't handle it, they will tell you. If you're concerned they won't tell you, monitor progress and their morale closely at the beginning to make sure they can. If there's resistance to take on more, spend some time finding out why. You may be able to help them find efficiencies and delegation opportunities for them, too. Think about how amazing your team, organization, and company can be if everyone is working at the highest level for their role. This offers tremendous growth for each individual as well as for the company!

When challenging clients to identify delegation opportunities, I often find that executives are resistant to delegating items they enjoy doing or items that are in their comfort zones. They find excuses for keeping the tasks or projects until I remove those excuses—and then they realize and admit they just don't want to delegate those items. After all, for many of us it's easier to focus on the tasks we know and are comfortable with rather than taking on new, riskier challenges. These tasks in our comfort zones become distractions from the perceived harder, higher-level projects we might be avoiding or are even fearful of. The focus on leadership and strategy can be daunting to some. It often requires us to work with less defined, more nebulous projects. Others may keep these delegable items for perceived job security reasons or concerns about not being needed. Be aware of items you're reluctant to delegate for personal reasons such as these. Challenge yourself to step up your game and the game of those in your organization.

The opportune time to delegate something is as soon as you receive it. Don't wait until it's getting close to the deadline and you realize you can't do it in time. By doing so, you hurt your staff's ability to manage their time effectively, and valuable time is potentially lost on this new task—not to mention it irritates your staff when something is delegated at the last minute. Remember, ask yourself the minute you receive a new task or project: *Who else can do this, should do this, or can help?* Then delegate it immediately if it's something that can and should be delegated. Don't forget to write yourself a reminder in your calendar to follow up.

Exhibit 3-a: Determining Delegation Opportunities

Ask yourself these questions when you create or receive a new task or project:

1. Am I the right person to be doing this task/project?
2. Who else can do this task/project?
3. Who should be able to do this task/project?
4. Who can learn and grow from this task/project?

The key to delegating effectively is clearly defining expectations. Make sure the recipient has a clear grasp of what you're asking for and when you expect it to be completed. Provide an outline, sample from the past, examples from other projects, or anything else you have that will help them understand the task. Provide the background for the task, including the reason for the task and the audience receiving it. This will help them make decisions, judgments, and assumptions on the task as needed. This will also help them understand the value of what they are doing. Have them play back for you in their words what they understand is needed and what the expectations are—to help ensure the expectations are clearly understood.

Exhibit 3-b: Information to Provide When Delegating

1. The purpose of the task/project

2. Outcome expected or decision to be made from the task/project?

3. What the completed task/project should look like (provide examples when possible)

4. The audience for the task/project

5. The deadlines and/or milestones

6. Ask the recipient what questions he or she has or expectations that need more clarity

When I worked with an executive vice president for a large global entertainment company, he complained about his staff not producing and meeting deadlines. I asked him to give me a recent example of how he delegated. He said that he told *so-and-so* to do *such-and-such* ASAP. I asked him what his definition of ASAP was. While he meant by the end of the next day, the recipient may have thought he meant by the end of the week. ASAP is a highly overused deadline that has lost its meaning in a world of fire drills and competing priorities.

Be clear about specific deadlines with a day and time. Better yet, a more effective way of giving deadlines is to let the recipients determine them when possible. Ask them when they think they can have a project done. More often than not, they will give themselves a tighter deadline but, more importantly, they will own it. They can't blame management for setting an unrealistic deadline. If the deadline is later than you anticipated, discuss what the competing priorities are and help them prioritize accordingly. If they say it will take longer than you think it should, it often means the expectations aren't clear. Readdress them. If it all has to be done, ask them what it will take to make it happen. They may need more resources (even temporarily) or forgiveness on other work. It's important that all expectations are clear and that discussions occur *beforehand* if there are any issues—rather than finding out at the time of the deadline that it couldn't be met. This also means one of the expectations of the recipient is to keep the delegator informed of any issues, competing priorities, or risks that could impact the task or project. Make sure all expectations are clear from the beginning.

Delegation provides another opportunity to grow your team and individuals within it. Challenge your team to take on more and higher-level projects. Before you give them a step-by-step procedure for getting the task done, ask them how *they* would approach it. This teaches them to think for themselves and—you never know—they may find a better way you hadn't thought of. Just make sure your expectations are clear. The more involved they are in taking on a project that has been delegated, the more they will own it and learn from it. Some of your team members will be more able to take a project and run with it. Some may require more direction. If the person you delegated to falls into the latter category, check in more often to make sure they're on track.

You can find more delegation opportunities by asking your employees what projects they would like to be involved in. Your high-potential, ambitious employees will jump at the chance to get involved in more challenging projects.

Keep in mind that just because you delegated something does not mean you relinquish responsibility and accountability. If it's a deliverable from your organization, you are still ultimately responsible. If the deadline or expectations are not met, you can't blame your people. *The buck stops here.* Don't wait until the end to find out something's going to be late, missing, or incorrect. Check in periodically on the progress of that task or project—as well as the other work the employee is responsible for—to be sure that nothing is falling through the cracks or falling behind and that priorities are clear. Some members of your organization will need more check-ins than others. Be mindful of that.

Finally, make sure you give credit and visibility to those you delegated work to. Let them present the work or at least be a part of the presentation. Publicly mention their names and the roles they played. This is a great way to recognize the work done and it provides incentive and motivation for your employees to ask for more opportunities. See exhibit 3-c for steps to effective delegation.

The results of effective delegation practices in an organization are visible. All employees are working at the appropriate levels with some stretch for new challenges and growth opportunities. There are no questions about who is responsible for doing what. Deadlines and milestones are clear and agreed upon. Expectations are met.

Exhibit 3-c: Steps to Effective Delegation

1. Delegate as soon as the task/project is created or received.

2. Provide the background of the task/project—purpose, audience, etc.

3. Clearly explain the expectations—what, when, etc.

4. Determine deadline(s).

5. Mark on your calendar when you need to follow up.

6. Provide visibility (when possible) and give credit for the work.

Summary

Delegation helps <u>executives</u> grow by raising the level of their work while raising the level of their employee's work. Executives will be able to focus on the larger, more strategic issues and problems, and their employees will have the opportunity to grow and learn as well.

Effective delegation helps a <u>company</u> grow by ensuring all levels are working at their highest levels and are being challenged to continue to grow. The value each employee brings will be maximized. The time higher-level executives spend on lower level tasks will be minimized so they can focus more on strategy and the future. Imagine how successful a company would be that had all employees working at their highest potentials!

CHAPTER 4:

· ·

Strategic Thinking

Strategic thinking is the bridge that links where you are to where you want to be.

—*John Maxwell*

The higher up a person is in an organization, the more time he or she should spend on *strategic thinking*. What is strategic thinking? Strategic thinking incorporates information from all around an organization to create a *bigger picture* framework that helps make decisions about the future of the organization. This information includes the strengths and weaknesses of the organization, risks and opportunities, economic environment, competitive and global marketplace, consumer trends, and the technological environment. Through the gathering and use of this information, an executive or business owner can predict future issues and opportunities and set the future direction of the organization.

I have coached many executives who have risen up the ranks in their organizations because of their accomplishments in their areas of expertise—typically more operational or task focused. When they get to a certain level of management they are expected to provide some strategic thought and direction, but many do not know how to do that. Many are uncomfortable with the things they need to do to be strategic—like researching and reading—because they're so worried it would be viewed as unproductive. After all, they're not producing anything—yet.

The impact of executives *not* providing strategic thought and input can be disastrous. There could be missed opportunities for new products, services, customers, technologies, and so forth. The competition can sneak up on you if you're not paying attention. Economic conditions can catch you off guard and ill-prepared. You can miss a technological improvement that will require a costly catch-up later. By not paying attention to the macro world around you and focusing on what needs to happen or change in the future, you put your organization and yourself at risk.

How does one practice the art of strategic thinking? You can start by reading, reading, and reading. The best way to stay current on the economic environment, competitive marketplace, technological and consumer trends—even leadership tools and practices—is to read. Some of the most successful executives attribute a big part of their success to the amount they read. Consider reading at least one of the popular periodicals like the *Wall Street Journal* or *Business Week*. Pay attention to the current popular business books like *Good to Great* by Jim Collins. Read the trade magazines for your particular industry or any others that significantly impact your organization or company. Ask others in your company or industry what they read to get ideas. I'm sure some of you are feeling overwhelmed at the thought of adding reading to your list of things to do. You'd be amazed at what you can learn by just reading the titles of the articles in the *Wall Street Journal*. You'll get an idea of which companies are in the news and why, or what's happening in the marketplace and economy. You don't have to read everything cover to cover. Prioritize articles with the most significance and relevance. The time you spend reading is well worth the investment.

Reading is considered research, but there is other research that can be done— with help from others. Research is a great project to delegate because it helps you gather information while including others in the process and teaching them to be strategic thinkers. Determine the data or information you need to help make decisions about the future. Share your reason for wanting to see the information and let others find the data. See exhibit 4-a for examples of data that might be helpful.

Exhibit 4-a: Data and Information for Strategic Decisions

a. Company information—trends, metrics, comparisons for key revenue and expense drivers

b. Competitor information—market share, price points, vendors, management teams, products, etc.

c. Marketplace information—technology, new opportunities, demand, risks, future challenges, products, etc.

d. Economy—future projections, interest rates, inflation rates, tax changes, regulation changes, political changes, etc.

e. Global—new marketplaces, expansion opportunities, offshore vendors, demographics, etc.

Another great way to find some innovative and creative strategic ideas is to let your natural curiosity have a voice. Think about the ideas you've had in your head about new products, processes, projects, and so on—and let them be heard and considered. We all know the importance of taking calculated risks to help with creativity and innovation, and this is a great start. Some great ideas have come about by people asking questions that start with "I wonder what would happen if we ... " Whether the topic is new ideas, resolving a problem, or finding a better way, let yours and others' curiosity help brainstorm solutions.

A common complaint, hurdle, or even excuse for not developing strategic thinking skills is *time*. How do we find the time to do it? It often gets put at the bottom of the list of priorities because it often doesn't solve an immediate need. This can be very shortsighted and many fall into this trap. Before you know it, you're behind your competitors or you've missed a golden opportunity. First, determine the time you should be allocating to strategic thinking. If you're a manager it may be 10 – 20 percent. A director may be 20 – 30 percent. VP's and above may be 50 percent or higher. A lot of it is determined by the function of your organization, state of your marketplace, and so on. I encourage you to have a dialogue with your boss, if necessary, to determine how much time should be spent on strategic thinking versus operational issues.

Once you determine how much of your time should be spent on strategic thinking, develop your goal. What do you want to focus on for the future? What projects will you create to achieve your goal? Keep in mind that a project can be just to research new opportunities. You are brainstorming at the highest levels so some ideas may not result in anything. This is where risk-taking is for executives. Just remember, staying static is a risk, too. Think about these potential opportunities:

New products
New customers
New information or data
New technologies
New processes
New services
New alliances or partnerships
New mergers or acquisitions
Divestitures
New related businesses

A word of caution: when reading and researching for new strategic opportunities, be careful and selective about which business *trend(s)* you choose to adopt. Business trends are the latest and greatest—popular business philosophies, ideas, initiatives, projects, and the like. Current and past examples include Management by Objective (MBO), Matrix Management, Total Quality Management (TQM), Business Process

Re-engineering, Six Sigma, Lean Manufacturing, Best Practices, and so on. Many of these trends are very good for some companies at certain times. Not every company can or *should* adopt all of them, however. Not only would it be impossible to successfully implement them all—or even more than one at a time—but to even *try* leads to confusion in the organization, significant inefficiencies, and high probability of failure to make any one of them successful.

I have worked with executives always interested in adopting the latest business trends. Unfortunately, none of these trendy ideas are completely implemented. The executives would get one started in the organization, not follow through, lose interest, and the initiative would fizzle out only to be replaced by another new one. Based on feedback in their 360 Assessments, their organizations were frustrated by the inefficiencies and lack of follow through, and confused by the different conflicting priorities. The executives were losing credibility with their organizations—who stopped paying much attention to the latest trendy initiatives the executives were trying to implement expecting those initiatives to eventually fizzle out, too. This can make it very difficult for these executives to carry out any new initiatives or projects.

If there are business trends you are interested in, carefully research and choose (with participation from relevant and key partners in the organization) the one you think would be the most relevant and valuable to your organization. Which one would contribute a positive return on investment and have a relatively high probability of success to adopt? Once the decision has been made, then *own it completely* and see it through.

Once you have determined what the new strategic projects are going to be, it's time to develop your plan. What are you going to delegate to create the time needed? Who should be involved in each project? What research needs to be done or what data needs to be collected? What approvals need to be obtained? What milestones will each project have in the short-term and long-term? What will you do weekly, in the short-term *and* in the long-term to focus on each project? How will you keep focus on existing targets while pursuing new ones? Create your plan, load the actions into your time management system, and make it happen!

Summary

Strategic thinking helps <u>executives</u> grow by allowing them time to focus on bigger picture issues, future opportunities, and challenges. Executives can find new opportunities to learn and add value to their organizations and resumes.

Strategic thinking helps <u>companies</u> grow by keeping some focus on the future. Existing and future economic, marketplace, technological, and competitive threats can be proactively addressed. New opportunities in products, services, technologies, and customers can be found.

CHAPTER 5:

•••••••••••••••••••••••••••••••••••••••

Building a Growth Team

No general can fight his battles alone. He must depend upon his lieutenants, and his success depends upon his ability to select the right man for the right place.

—Philip Armour

Your success as a leader or business owner is significantly dependent on how well you can build and maintain a strong team. After all, the people you are leading are the ones producing. Your job is to pave the way for success—to keep the organization focused on targets, give direction and guidance for the future, provide the tools and environment that offers the optimum productivity, remove road blocks that get in the way, and provide development opportunities to leverage and grow the talent. It's also your job to build a team not only capable of doing the work, but capable of adding more value, maximizing the potential of the organization, and helping it grow, too. Top talent with top leadership leads to top teams; top teams lead in turn to top organizations, which lead to top companies. Be on top!

All too often I hear executives complain of their inability to meet goals or grow their organizations because of the shortcomings of their staff. This is in the control of the executives and, if it's not, it should be made to be. Underperforming employees need to step up, be trained or be removed. Clear expectations not being met are unacceptable. As a leader, you are only as good as your team. Creating a growth team is your number one priority.

The first step in building a growth team is *hiring* a growth team. The first step to hiring a growth team is to understand whom you need to hire. Hiring the wrong person for a position can be costly to a company, not only in the hiring process and investment in the new employee, but also the opportunity cost of not having the right person maximizing productivity and adding value. Then there's the cost and time it takes removing the wrong person. This is why the hiring process is so critical.

The pre-hiring process prepares for hiring the right person. The product of the pre-hiring process is a detailed job description. This job description is used not only externally for recruiting purposes, but also internally to clearly establish the skills, experience, personalities, and educational background required. The more detailed the job description, the better your chances of hiring the right person. Unfortunately, this step is often overlooked or is approached as a corporate or procedural requirement versus a valuable tool to help ensure a successful hire.

When creating the job description, get input from others—others who hold similar jobs, internal or external customers of the role, and others who will interact with this position. This will help create a well-rounded job description that incorporates the needs of people who will be interacting with the new hire. If you're struggling to think of the requirements of the job—including the soft skills required and attributes that make a candidate a good fit—do some research on the computer by looking up similar job descriptions. Look at job descriptions posted on your company's website or other companies' websites for ideas. There are also many search sites available for researching job descriptions. Consult with your HR representative, if you have one, who should also be able to help.

Once you have a completed job description, you're ready for the search process. There are many ways to find candidates. Start internally by talking to others about potential internal candidates. Use your network as a source for candidates. Depending on the level and difficulty in finding candidates, professional headhunters might make sense. There are many places to post your open position for attracting candidates. If your company has a job board, make sure it's posted there. Consider the available search sites to post the job and which ones make sense for the position. There are the larger sites like CareerBuilder, and more targeted sites for executives only, specific industries, or specific functions (sales, finance, and so forth). LinkedIn has become a popular place to post open positions and find good candidates.

Once the resumes start rolling in, have been weeded through, and potential candidates have been identified, the next step to a successful hire is in the job interview process. Before interviews begin, it's important to set up the interview process. This includes establishing who will conduct initial interviews to find the candidates with the most potential for hire and who will comprise the team of interviewers to conduct subsequent rounds of interviews. Then conduct a quick kick-off meeting for each open position to make sure everyone doing the interviewing is on the same page with regard to the requirements and expectations of the job. This is a great opportunity to answer any questions about the job or potential candidates as well. I can remember going through job interviews and getting frustrated by the different messages I received about the job requirements or expectations from the different interviewers. This can leave a candidate confused about what is required or what the job will be like. While the interview questions will hopefully be different from each interviewer, the job expectations should be consistent and clear.

Before interviews begin, some time should be spent on assessing the interviewing skills of the interviewers. This is often an area of management skill deficiency, yet it is key to hiring the right person the first time. Many of us have never taken classes or received formal training in the fine art of interviewing. The interviewing process is not only for vetting the right skills, experience, education, and background, but also it is for determining the right fit in terms of personality. It's also important to assess how well the position matches what candidates are looking for in their next role and to share information about the role and the company with the candidates so they can do the same. Otherwise, you might hire someone who quickly becomes frustrated and unhappy and is soon looking for another job again. Thoughtful consideration should be given to the questions that are asked to ascertain all of the above. Once a candidate is hired after a thorough interviewing process, there should be few and small surprises for the company and the candidate. If any of the interviewers are determined to have weak interviewing skills, they should be appropriately trained or coached prior to the interviewing process.

Since the hiring process is so important, it can be long, time-consuming, and expensive. You can keep the costs and time consumption down by having an initial interview to find only the best candidates who will move forward with more interviews. This first screener should be capable and trusted to determine who moves forward in the interview process. If the screener doesn't see a fit with a candidate, the process for that candidate should stop there. Too often interviews are set up so candidates meet multiple people right after the screener so, whether or not the screener approves the candidate, the candidate is interviewed by others wasting valuable time for the other interviewers. If a candidate doesn't pass the initial screen, end the interviews there.

To help conduct effective interviews, think ahead about the questions you're going to ask. The most effective questions require a candidate to share previous experiences that relate to the challenges of the job. Open-ended questions offer the candidate opportunities to embellish on the questions, which is where the interviewer will find the most information and get a sense of the candidate's personality and fit.

After the interviews have been completed for each candidate, regroup with all of the interviewers and discuss each one. You might have each interviewer rank the candidates. Ask what each interviewer liked or disliked about each. Determine what questions or concerns they have about any of the candidates.

Using references in a job search has become more difficult. It is harder to get valuable information from the references due to their fear of saying something negative and being sued for defamation or slander. I still suggest calling them. If you have an HR department available, utilize them for checking credentials and educational backgrounds. Call the references and ask questions like: "Has this employee illustrated these skills or had this experience?" In some cases you might get a reference willing to provide some additional information. It's always worth a try. This is an area where having a network can pay off. You might know someone who has worked with the candidate— or know someone who knows someone who has worked with him or her and can get information on the candidate's reputation. Some HR departments are now using LinkedIn to find information on a candidate. They contact people the candidate has linked to in their previous company—people who may not be on the list of references.

The time spent creating a clear job description, preparing for the interview process, and checking references is an investment well spent. You'll avoid hiring the wrong person—which can be costly and time-consuming—and you'll reap the benefits of hiring the right person.

Once you have hired the candidate you assess to be the right person for the job, it's up to you to set him or her up for success. You can do that by clearly articulating what the *expectations* are. Describe what success looks like so the employee can achieve it. Whether you have metrics to gauge performance, a list of deliverables to be achieved, or goals to accomplish—the clearer the expectations, the better the chance the new employee can meet them.

The same holds true for existing employees, which leads me to the next topic—goal setting. Expectations and goals should be clear and agreed upon every step of the way. This is why I'm a big believer in annual goal setting as part of a performance review process. While many see annual goal setting as an exercise to make *corporate* happy or just another process they are "supposed" to do, they are also missing a valuable opportunity. Annual goal setting allows you to establish clearly defined and agreed-upon goals, to find growth opportunities for the individual as well as the organization and company, and to hold the employees accountable to what is expected, just like you will be. Employees want to know what is expected of them. How can they achieve success if they don't know what is considered success?

When creating goals for the individuals on your team, look at the vision you established and goals set for your organization. Determine how each individual can help achieve the vision and organizational goals through his or her individual goals. For example, if the organization has a metric goal to achieve, what part of that should each employee contribute? If the goal is to improve relationships with another organization, each employee's goals might include the same at the individual level. The goals of the individuals in an organization should reflect the goals of the organization.

An employee's goals should focus on the individual's strengths and weaknesses. How can the individual leverage his or her strengths and shore up weaknesses? This will help the employee grow, and the organization and company will benefit from it. These goals should be created with the employee. The more you can involve the employees in the setting of their goals, the more they will accept and own them. In fact, I suggest you ask the employees what goals they can set for themselves to achieve their growth. They're more likely to own, buy in, and get excited about goals they help create.

While having goals in general is important, having the *right* goals is just as important. Make sure the annual goals of an individual include everything he or she will be held accountable for, including any numeric metrics and behavioral goals. Goals should include any communication, team building, and relationship building skills. After all, in most positions an employee's ability to work with others has a direct impact on how successful he or she will be. It is more difficult to clearly articulate the softer, behavioral goals but this shouldn't dissuade you. It's still worth the effort as it helps maintain focus and motivation on those goals.

These days, few of us can be successful on our own. It takes teams, relationships, and (often) heavy communication to be successful. This is why the goals for behavioral skills are just as important as the more quantifiable ones. On many occasions I have heard clients complain that certain expectations are not being met. Typically, they are behavioral in nature. My first question is whether or not these expectations are included in their annual goals. Often they are not. By clearly documenting all expectations, you help remove any doubt about what is expected. Documenting the expectations in the annual goals will help reiterate the importance of each goal and the expectations that will be discussed in performance reviews. You also have something in writing to gauge performance against—and to which—you can hold employees accountable. If the employee is bonus-eligible, incorporating these expectations in annual goals will be even more powerful as their lack of achieving these expectations may hit their wallet at the end of the year.

An individual's goals might include behaviors and values the organization or company is trying to focus on. It's not uncommon to have *leadership competencies* or *core competencies* within an organization. These have become more prevalent in recent years as companies put more focus on behavioral skills. They might include teamwork, integrity, management, influence, innovation, leadership, communication, diversity, strategic thinking, and so forth. If your company or organization has specific leadership competencies or core competencies, then make sure the annual goals and performance reviews reflect them.

While we're talking about establishing and meeting expectations and goals, let's talk about the best way to do that on an ongoing basis— weekly meetings. You should be having weekly one-on-one meetings with each of your direct reports. This not only provides an opportunity to reinforce expectations and gauge progress, it also helps build relationships with your people and keep your finger on the pulse on the business, too. As much as people moan and groan about yet another meeting, this particular meeting typically is well-received (if not much-desired) and can offer big payback in productivity, communication, and employee morale. In the 360's I've done for executives, this is the most common request from employees—more face-time with the boss. In fact, I have yet to receive feedback requesting less time. It doesn't have to be long—even half an hour or less if that works—but it must be consistent and a priority. Too often executives set up these meetings but then let other meetings or projects override them. This doesn't help you fulfill the purpose of these meetings and can be detrimental because you're sending a message to your people that they are not considered a priority. The subject of meetings will be covered in more detail in chapter 8.

Once the expectations have been established, as the leader you must hold employees *accountable*. In many organizations I have seen what seems to be an epidemic lack of accountability. It starts from the top and cascades down. It leads to missed deadlines, inaccurate information, poor performance, poor products or services, and eventually a diminished ability to compete. If employees don't take accountability seriously internally, you can bet they have the same attitude externally with customers. Accountability can never be compromised. Everyone in the organization from the top down must be held accountable for his or her responsibilities and expectations. Accountability has to be part of the culture.

Accountability is achieved through immediate and constant feedback. If something is missed, it must be dealt with immediately. If you've set a deadline for someone, schedule a reminder for yourself in your time management system to follow up when it's due. Even if you no longer need it at that particular time, at least follow up and discuss it. If deadlines pass with no acknowledgement, employees will start expecting latitude with all deadlines. It's human nature. They will expect future behaviors based on past behaviors. If changes happen along the way—either with deadlines or any other expectations—communicate them immediately. It can be very demotivating to employees for them to work hard toward a deadline or requirement only to find out after the fact that it wasn't needed or used at that time.

Things happen. We all know that some deadlines or expectations may not be met 100 percent. Make it clear that any concerns regarding the ability to meet expectations need to be brought to your attention immediately so you can make decisions and adjustments, or manage others' expectations early— not at the time something is due. Surprises are not acceptable, as they won't be to your boss, board, or customers.

Lack of accountability leads to mediocrity, at best. If you work with your team to set stretch goals but realistic expectations, communicate those expectations well, follow up as needed, provide support, and be diligent about accountability—then you and your team will accomplish more than you thought possible. Your employees will grow, you will grow, and your organization will grow. Exhibit 5-a provides the formula for setting expectations and enforcing accountability.

Exhibit 5-a: Expectations and Accountability Formula
- Collaboratively set stretch goals but realistic expectations.
- Over-communicate those expectations.
- Constantly and consistently reinforce the expectations.
- Follow up and provide feedback and support.
- Be diligent about accountability to those expectations.
- Celebrate the success!

Specific goals that are particularly important to the company—or important for an executive to achieve—should have financial incentives attached. The goals might be quantitative results, like achieving revenue or profit targets, margins, or inventory levels. They might be based on metrics, like customer satisfaction or safety standards. Strategic goals for the company might include successfully working with another division to create a new product (which will help break down silos to be discussed in chapter 6). Behavioral goals might include improving time management skills, collaboration, executive presence, building relationships, or strategic thinking.

I am often asked for help with motivating executives on specific goals they are not achieving because they are not focusing enough attention on them, even though these goals are important to their companies. The first question I ask is whether or not the executives' compensations are tied to these important goals. Typically, they're not. Tying compensation to goals is a great way to get the appropriate attention and focus on these specific, important goals for the company.

Consistently missed deadlines or expectations, especially when they occur without warning, should be addressed aggressively. First, find out why the deadlines are being missed. If the reason is something that can be fixed, do so. It might require something like changing priorities or adding resources; then continue to monitor performance. If deadlines continue to be missed, appropriate disciplinary actions need to begin. Start with verbal warnings and if the problem continues, move to written warnings and, finally, termination. You are only as good as your people and the output they produce. If they're not meeting expectations, they have to go. This also provides a clear message throughout your organization of what is expected, thereby promoting the importance of accountability.

Leaders are expected to be change agents. Through their strategic thinking they help create and lead new projects that respond to the changing environment around and within their organizations. They have to rely on their organizations to make these changes and projects successful. As change agents they need to identify the supporters of the projects and the blockers of the change. The supporters should be developed and motivated. The naysayers and blockers should first be given the opportunity to become supporters, but if they don't, they need to go. Naysayers and blockers cannot only be detrimental to any change efforts; they can completely kill any attempts to be successful.

In addition to constant and immediate feedback, I am a big believer in annual *performance reviews*. This provides a great opportunity to check in on those annual goals established earlier. It also allows the leader and the employee to spend some time focusing on performance and growth. Performance reviews too often get put at the bottom of a list of projects. This not only hurts the leader's ability to monitor performance and constantly look for growth, it also leads the employee to believe he or she is not important. By having an annual review process, it puts that topic at the top of the list for a period of time and focuses on the people. Employees want feedback. They want to know whether or not they're doing a good job and what they can do to perform better. They also want to know what their growth opportunities are and what they need to do to achieve them.

Leaders who consider performance reviews a waste of time—as just another corporate requirement or paperwork for merit planning—are missing the point. This exercise is not just to let corporate know it's been done or to put another check mark on the list of to-do's. It's an opportunity to focus on the individuals in the team, take stock of the talents in the group, look for opportunities to leverage strengths, and discuss the weaknesses that need to be shored up. It provides an opportunity for your employees to focus on how to leverage their individual strengths and work on the weaknesses. It helps you and the employees focus on growth opportunities at the individual and group level.

Performance reviews should be given as much time and attention as any other project in the company. They should be treated seriously and given a high priority, after all, your employees are your most important assets and are critical to your success. I used to work from home a day or two just to focus on the performance reviews. I had too many interruptions at my office and wanted to devote all of my time and attention to the reviews. I have seen other executives do the same.

Performance reviews should not just include praise and accomplishments. Many executives feel compelled to do this to make an employee feel good or perhaps avoid conflict. Either way, it's a disservice to the employee. Performance reviews need to include growth opportunities. Everyone can grow, even top performers. Most employees want to know where they can grow in developing skills, gaining experience, or obtaining more knowledge. Our jobs as leaders are to help point out those opportunities and help guide our employees in achieving them.

The topics in the performance review should coincide with the annual goals established earlier. There shouldn't be any surprises on topics the employee is being evaluated on. In other words, new goals the employee was not aware of cannot be added as a topic to be evaluated against in that performance review. It can, however, become a new goal to start focusing on from that point. No previously established goals should be excluded either. All goals should be discussed to reinforce accountability. There shouldn't be any surprises with feedback either. Feedback should be provided all year long; employees shouldn't be hearing feedback for the first time during the performance review. The performance review provides an opportunity to review that feedback, acknowledge improvements already observed, and set future goals to continue to address them.

Different formats used for performance reviews will resonate with different employees. Numbers-oriented employees probably prefer rating scales, while others prefer written remarks. I suggest doing both for each category employees are rated on. A rating scale helps put the feedback in perspective, while written comments add context and more details. The comments should include what the employee has done well and where the employee should focus for improvements and growth. It's human nature to focus on what is perceived as the *negative* comments. If you start the feedback in that light it can make the whole area of feedback seem negative. Always start with a positive comment about what the employee has done well or improved upon. Focus on the future for the growth opportunities. It's not about harping on the past but rather on focusing on changes and growth for the future. For example, rather than saying, "You did *x* wrong," you might say, "In the future, practice doing *y*." Be specific with examples as much as possible for both positive and negative feedback. Finally, end the category with a positive encouraging note about the opportunities for growth and development.

The most powerful and comprehensive performance reviews incorporate feedback with a 360-degree view. It starts with a self-review completed by the employees. This gives employees an opportunity to highlight the achievements they feel they've made and to recognize (and therefore *own*) the areas they think they can grow in. Then it includes feedback from employees' subordinates, peers, bosses, and even internal or external customers. This feedback can be gathered through phone calls or short questionnaires. While this approach of gathering this feedback takes longer, it's well worth the effort. Leaders don't know (nor *should* they know) what an employee does all day and how he or she relates to others. We've all seen employees who manage up well but have frustrated peers or employees below them. This approach will bring that to light. The final, formal written performance review incorporates feedback from every perspective—that of the employee, peers, bosses, and any other relevant parties.

Most larger companies have performance reviews that require the signatures of the employees receiving the reviews and supervisors providing them. This practice helps protect the employee, supervisors, and the company from any misunderstandings regarding expectations and performance. Copies are then kept in the employees' files.

Performance reviews are never a substitute for ongoing, immediate feedback. Both positive and negative feedback should always be provided immediately. *Immediately* does not mean within a month or even a week. Ideally, feedback should be provided within twenty-four hours. I have had many clients put off providing negative feedback with a variety of excuses. More often than not they are just avoiding the difficult conversation. Keep in mind that negative feedback is less about reprimanding employees and more about correcting an issue and/or helping them learn and grow. Most employees want to hear feedback right away so they can continue doing what's working or make corrections on what's not working.

When providing any kind of negative feedback, be sure to focus on the *behavior* versus criticizing the *person*. If you identify the behavior and focus on that, it makes it clear to the person receiving it exactly what needs to change. For example, saying, "You're too aggressive" to someone leaves it up to the person to figure out what that means and interpret when he or she is doing it—versus saying, "When you [do *x* behavior] it comes across to some as being too aggressive." Focusing on the behavior is also easier to hear and accept by the recipient because it's taken less personally or less as a criticism about who he or she is as a person. Negative feedback is also easier to give and receive if it's focused on the future desired behavior and not on the past mistakes. Rather than saying, "You've been too aggressive," you might say, "In the future you might consider [preferred behavior] to help your teambuilding and relationship-building skills." Negative feedback should include a discussion about how to address the issue or growth opportunity so the employee can work on it right away and have some guidance from you on how to do it.

While conducting 360 Assessments for executives, a common request I hear from their employees is for more immediate feedback—both positive and negative. I recently facilitated a meeting with middle level executives (directors, vice presidents, and senior vice presidents) for an organization in one of the largest entertainment companies about how to stay motivated. I conducted an anonymous survey to obtain information that provided the agenda for that meeting. One of the key topics that created a lot of discussion was about providing and receiving immediate feedback. It was considered one of the most desired yet the most lacking motivator for this organization, and not just up and down the organization, but across between peers as well!

While the importance of providing immediate negative feedback is more obvious, providing immediate positive feedback is less so and, therefore, often forgotten. It's easier to see the impact of providing negative feedback because hopefully it results in change that can be seen. The motivation and goodwill provided by positive feedback is harder to identify. Providing immediate positive feedback is not only a big motivator for most employees, it also helps reinforce the skills and behaviors that are working, too. Providing that feedback publicly, or in front of others, can be a learning experience for the audience as well.

When coaching executives of employees looking for more positive feedback, I often suggest the executives look for opportunities on a daily or weekly basis—depending on the size of their organizations—to provide positive feedback. At the end of every day or week, ask yourself which employees did a good job that day or week and let them know. This practice will help you focus on positive feedback and identify opportunities for it. Look beyond just your organization. Look across at peers and even up for opportunities to recognize accomplishments. Everyone loves to hear positive feedback, and it can help infuse some positive energy into your organization. The feedback and compliments have to be authentic, though, or they won't be taken seriously. If you can't find opportunities to provide positive feedback on at least a weekly basis, consider whether or not you have a high potential or growth organization. If everyone complimented one other person every day for something well done, imagine the impact that could have on motivation and a culture!

Any feedback should be delivered face-to-face if at all possible, particularly performance reviews. Just like in written form, any verbal feedback should start and end with positive remarks. Avoid getting into disputes about details in performance reviews. Remind the receiver of the feedback that it is based on perception and often *perception is reality.*

If they disagree with anything in the review, they need to focus on what behaviors are driving the perception and work on that. The end of the review should be a discussion and agreement about next year's goals. And the process starts again.

Jack Welch, former CEO of GE, had a policy at GE to rank the employees of every organization each year and fire the bottom 10 percent every year, as described in his book *Jack: Straight from the Gut*. While that may seem harsh, it is very effective at building strong teams comprised of top talent. It also keeps a natural competitiveness between employees if they know they will be ranked compared to others and could lose their jobs if they don't keep up with the rest. It also prevents employees from getting too comfortable or complacent.

In every organization I have worked with, as an employee in my earlier career and later as a coach, I have seen how executives and organizations get held back when they keep lackluster employees. My point is this: if you have employees with subpar performance, address it right away. Document the subpar performance immediately. Include in that documentation plans that outline expectations and corrective actions required with deadlines. Monitor progress against those plans. If performance is not brought up to expectations, the employees should be terminated. Terminate consistent underperformers expediently. These days I hear about human resources and legal departments getting in the way of terminating employees due to liability concerns for protected classes. As long as you have your documentation done including all verbal and written warnings, you should be able to appropriately terminate the employees. If HR or Legal has concerns, find out what needs to be done and work with them to make it happen. Keeping poor performers should never be an option. I've gone to battle with both departments more than once, made my case and convinced them I needed to terminate underperformers. Again, as long as the documentation is solid, terminating underperformers is the right decision for the company. Often terminating underperformers can be good for those terminated, as well. It gives them an opportunity to find positions they are better suited for, can perform better in, and can potentially be happier in. Be aggressive about building and maintaining the right team.

Summary

<u>Executives</u> grow by building growth teams. Their opportunities for success are increased, time spent on poor performers is decreased, and focus on important, more strategic issues and opportunities is maximized.

<u>Companies</u> grow through the building of growth teams because when the right employees are hired for the right jobs and given opportunities to grow, it raises the level of success and opportunities for the entire company.

CHAPTER 6:

● ●

Participatory & Collaborative Management

Leadership should be more participative than directive, more enabling than performing.

—*Mary D. Poole*

As employees climb the ranks to executive positions, they often feel pressure that they are expected to have all the answers. After all, if they're *that* good to be promoted to an executive position, they should have all the answers, right? Wrong. Quite the contrary— the most successful executives understand that they don't and *shouldn't* have all the answers. Executives can't know everything required in order to make decisions. They rely on their teams to help. Executives know what questions to ask to help gather the right information, promote creative thinking for problem solving, and gauge how well the overall company is doing. They may make the final call on decisions, but rarely is it made without input from others. Also, consider this: executives are often the furthest removed from where the action occurs. The employees "in the trenches" are closest to the action and therefore can offer the best perspective on how decisions will impact the company. They are also in the best positions to offer ideas on what can be improved, developed, or made more efficient. Their thoughts and ideas should be carried up the chain of command if not directly then at least through management.

Those who think they should have all the answers tend to be closed to other ideas. They don't want to appear weak if someone else's ideas are used. Or they have the mistaken thought that they are the smartest people in the room and therefore will always have the best ideas. If you're the smartest person in the room, you're not hiring well. Your goal should be to hire people smarter than you in their given fields of expertise.

Executives who make all the decisions and *direct* rather than *lead* are holding down their organizations, putting risk in their decisions, and probably hurting employee morale. Employees want to participate in decisions they can add value to and/or decisions that impact them. This offers opportunities for growth and promotes buy-in and ownership in the decisions. Employees are typically closer to the action and have more relevant information to base decisions on. According to Adult Learning Theory as described by Malcolm Knowles, adults don't like to be told what to do and will resist it. Give them the opportunity to participate and the result will be better decisions that are more easily adopted.

As a leader, your job is to inspire creative thought and productivity. The more you engage others in decision making and creative problem solving, the more likely you'll come up with the best decisions. You'll also be helping members of your team grow as they learn to think critically and creatively about solutions. The decisions will also be more likely to be bought into and owned by them because they were part of the process.

Another advantage to having a participative and collaborative approach is that it promotes open communication up from the organization for input and feedback. I continue to be amazed at the executives who don't receive honest input and feedback from their direct reports because that culture has not been cultivated. This creates organizations of employees who tell the executives what they want to hear rather than giving them their true opinions. This is a dangerous situation for executives because they could be making decisions without all the information, support, or buy-in. I have seen many bad decisions made in a vacuum this way, based on one person's knowledge and opinion alone, with fake agreement and buy-in by others. If you find your people are agreeing with you all of the time, you may have this type of organization. As much as you would love to believe it's really because everyone thinks you're right all the time, there's a good chance that you are just not getting honest opinions and feedback.

How do you get honest opinions and feedback? Many executives complain that they ask for it but don't get it. The organization may already have developed a fear of sharing feedback. Changing that will take time but it can and should be done. First, you have to be open to receiving feedback—and truly open, not just going through the motions. You have to be willing to hear, accept, and appreciate all feedback no matter how hard it is to hear or even how much you agree or disagree with it. The old adage is true—*perception is reality*—so whatever you may disagree with may be reality for those who perceive it.

Now you have to ask for the feedback. The same rule applies for asking questions—keep them open-ended to get the best results. Closed, or *yes/no* questions make it too easy for people to just answer and provide the feedback they think you want to hear. Some examples of questions include: "How could we have handled this differently to achieve better results?" and "What do you think is the best solution for this problem?" or "How can I improve my perception as a leader?" It may take some prodding to get answers, but keep at it. You have to build that trust in the organization and build the culture of feedback. As you receive feedback, play back what you hear and ask clarifying questions to make sure you understand the intended message. Don't argue or justify your position. The purpose right now is to get information. Don't be defensive. Thank the feedback provider for their feedback even if you don't agree with it. You don't have to agree; just be appreciative. You can say, "Thank you for that feedback—I'll take that into consideration," or "I'll give that some thought." The moment you get defensive or disagree with the feedback provider, you have, in essence, tried to discredit the feedback. The provider will feel that they were not heard or their opinion was not respected and may never provide honest feedback again.

There are some risks in asking for feedback, ideas, and input. When asking for feedback on your leadership abilities, it could be seen as insecure or weak if you ask too often and too many people (unless it's a structured 360 Assessment). That's why you should be thoughtful about whom you ask for input and on which topics. Also, if you decide not to follow up on any of the ideas or input, the providers could become disappointed and unmotivated to provide any more. If you see this as a risk with any of your direct reports, it can be mitigated by recognizing the input and explaining why you are going another direction. Then the provider will feel heard, which is the most important part.

A great tool and resource for obtaining feedback is the 360 Assessment introduced in chapter 1. There are many off-the-shelf assessments, and there are quantitative and qualitative assessments (surveys and questionnaires). The most effective and powerful of the 360 Assessments are the interview style evaluations conducted by an outside consultant or coach. A qualified and experienced consultant or coach can dive deeply into focused areas for detailed input, protect confidentiality for the participants, and gather highly-valuable, specific, feedback.

There is a lot to be gained by *collaborating* with peers. I have had many clients receive feedback through 360 Assessments that they appear to their peers to always have to have the answers, speak first, or get so invested in their opinions that they don't seem open to others' opinions or ideas. This has created dissension, distrust, and an air of negative or unproductive competition with peers.

First, let's define *collaboration* in this context. Collaborating with peers includes the following: asking for ideas, thoughts and input; allowing peers to participate in decisions or projects that impact them; and brainstorming solutions rather than assuming you have them all.

Leaders who make decisions that impact other leaders without their input are not building relationships and promoting teamwork. The decisions will be resisted and walls will build between the organizations. Proactively include peers on decisions that impact them to search for the best solutions, promote buy-in, and reduce resistance. This is another great opportunity to ask those powerful, thought-provoking *what* and *how* questions to elicit ideas and thoughts. Collaborating with peers will help proactively and subtly achieve buy-in from them on projects and decisions that impact them. If you collaborate on an idea with a peer who may not be impacted by the decision, the peer can still provide support. For example, your boss or even your staff may ask your peer for an opinion on something you're doing. If they've been even peripherally involved, they are more likely to provide supportive comments when asked. If you collaborate with your peers, they are more likely to reciprocate. This will provide opportunities for you to be involved and influence areas outside of your immediate scope. You will also be more proactively informed about what's going on in other areas of the company. All of this breeds teamwork and, more importantly, trust.

If your peer is not asking for your participation or collaboration on something that impacts you, how can you get involved? If they're not asking for your input, chances are they won't be open to it. As a general rule, adults don't listen to opinions or ideas they didn't ask for. So offering your idea may not be well received. Try these two approaches. Find a way to be asked to be involved. You might offer resources, information, or other forms of help but it must be genuine. If it comes across calculated, it will backfire. You can also ask those powerful, open-ended questions. Ask "How will this idea or decision impact my organization?" or "How can I or my organization help?" Again, the questions must be genuine and sincere, which means your intent must be genuine and sincere.

One of the most common—yet detrimental—conditions in an organization is one in which silos are built between people, departments, or divisions within a company. This is the result of individuals and/or organizations putting their interests before those of the company and protecting their domain. I continue to be amazed at the number of companies that experience and suffer from this. This phenomenon starts from the top— with leaders reluctant to work with their peers—and trickles down the organization. It results in lost collaboration as people don't share ideas or information, solve problems together, or find ways to work better together. Silos can lead to significant inefficiencies because they create a more formal environment with more meetings and documentation required. It can take longer to get decisions made and for changes to be implemented. It often leads to redundancies with organizations doing duplicative work in efforts to control something—or from just not knowing other organizations are doing the same things. Silos can result in lost opportunities for the company as departments or divisions don't share ideas or work together to create new opportunities. Having silos can hurt a company's ability to adjust to the competitive landscape. New processes are difficult to implement, and developing new products can take too long—hindering a company's ability to stay competitive.

A great example of the damaging effects of an environment with silos happened at Sony as described in the book *Steve Jobs* by Walter Isaacson. As Apple entered and eventually dominated the music distribution industry with iTunes and the iPod, it was a lost opportunity for Sony. Sony had the opportunity to own this market because they had the technology capabilities as well as the access to the content through their music division. Unfortunately for Sony, the silos were so strong the divisions couldn't work together to develop a new music distribution platform and service. This gave Apple plenty of time to do it.

While promoting the idea of collaboration and participation, we can't lose the spirit of healthy debate. We're not trying to build an organization of people that just agree with each other all the time. That can be detrimental to an organization, as it doesn't offer new and broader ideas—or the challenging of existing ones. What we're building is an organization of trust so everyone is free to provide thoughts, ideas, and constructive criticism. This is what helps get to the best idea generation and creative problem solving. See exhibit 6-a for the attributes of healthy debates.

Exhibit 6-a: Attributes of Healthy Debates

1. Participants have an open mind.

2. Pre-conceived notions are ignored.

3. Judgments are not made.

4. There is freedom to express constructive opinions.

5. Ideas are challenged.

6. Questions are asked to help gather relevant information and further the thought process.

7. Mutual respect is exhibited.

8. Participants agree to disagree, when necessary.

How do you develop a participatory and collaborative style? Start by having a genuine desire to get input and ideas from others. Recognize that you may not have the best answers, solutions, and ideas all the time. Follow your natural curiosity about other ideas and thoughts. Be willing to seek more from others in search of the best by inspiring creative thinking from all. The best way to do this is to ask powerful, open-ended questions that promote—and, dare I say, *provoke*—deeper thinking. These power questions help further the thinking of everyone involved. Remember, most of the questions start with either *how* or *what*. For example: "How do we achieve x given these challenges?"; "What would happen if y?"; and "What new ideas do we have about z?" The questions must be authentic, with a genuine desire for input; the answers must be received with an open mind. The minute you disagree with, dismiss, or criticize an idea or thought, you've shut down the creative thinking. If you find yourself dismissing or disagreeing, ask another question to help validate your concerns or lead others to reach the same conclusion on their own. This is a skill I have seen mastered by successful executives. It not only helps find the best solutions and ideas, but also creates an inclusive environment people enjoy working in because their thoughts and ideas are sought, listened to, considered, and appreciated.

The key to a successful participatory and collaborative approach is balancing including others with not holding up the decision or process. Those who take the collaborative approach to the extreme seek consensus on *all* decisions. This creates a bottleneck, delays decisions or processes, and can make the executive appear weak because they can't seem to make a decision. Having a haphazard approach about seeking input from whoever crosses your path may not be effective either. Be thoughtful and strategic about whom you include in decisions. See exhibit 6-b, Determining Decision Participants.

Exhibit 6-b: Determining Decision Participants
- Can this decision be delegated (with my oversight)? To whom?
- Who has information pertinent to this decision?
- Who will be impacted by this decision?
- Whose opinion do I trust in these circumstances?
- Who can be an advocate for this decision?
- Who is appropriate to include in this decision?
- Who can learn from participating in making this decision?

While a participatory and collaborative style of decision-making is preferred, there are occasions when it is not feasible or appropriate. Urgent circumstances that require immediate decisions may have to be directed by you. Personnel decisions regarding your direct reports may need to be made unilaterally. Highly sensitive or confidential decisions may limit your ability to include others. Be mindful of the circumstances and time available to include others in making decisions. One way to help identify when a directive approach is appropriate is to ask yourself the following three questions that I call *the Three Es*:

1. Is the situation an *emergency?*
2. Are you setting *expectations?*
3. Are you the *expert?*

If the answer is *yes* to any of these questions, then a directive approach is appropriate. Otherwise you might consider a more collaborative approach allowing you to lead versus direct.

A powerful approach to leading others is through a coaching style. This style is accomplished by asking those powerful, open-ended (how, what) questions that help others think through decisions or solutions rather than just wait for direction or answers. This not only allows those you're leading to participate, it also promotes buy-in and provides an opportunity for them to learn how to think on their own, too. Then next time they'll be able to come up with solutions on their own. Exhibit 6-c provides examples of these open-ended questions.

Exhibit 6-c: Examples of Open-Ended Questions
- If you were making this decision on your own, what would it be? Based on what?
- What are the options?
- What information do you need to make this decision?
- What do you know about the circumstances? What don't you know?
- What's the best-case scenario? What's the worst-case scenario?
- If you could do anything about this, regardless of risk, what would it be?

Summary

Executives can grow by adapting a participatory and collaborative management style because it allows them to hear new ideas and acquire more information for making decisions. Risks are reduced, buy-in becomes easier, and new opportunities can be discovered.

Companies can grow when participatory and collaborative management styles are used because decisions are made with more and better information, risks are reduced, teamwork is enhanced, employee morale is increased, new opportunities can be found, and implementation becomes easier.

CHAPTER 7:

• •

Communication

Precision of communication is important, more important than ever, in our era of hair trigger balances, when a false or misunderstood word may create as much disaster as a sudden thoughtless act.

—*James Thurber*

C ommunication skills are not just important in business; they are important in life. As people have gotten busier and rely more on technology that allows for and almost encourages shorthand communication (email and texting), communication skills have suffered. People often feel rushed, so they talk faster or write a quick note and move on to the next thing. Less thought is being put into who the audience is, how the message might be received, and what the other person may be saying. Written communication is often now in short form whether as email, texts, Twitter messages, Facebook posts, and so forth. Again, the messages are often not thought through, and there are abbreviations made that can confuse the messages even further. The results are misunderstood messages leading to errors, misinformed decisions, hurt feelings, and damaged relationships. In the business world, poor communication can also lead to difficult work environments, inefficiencies, poor morale, and hits to the bottom line.

In my executive coaching practice, I see how communication skills impact executives' abilities to lead effectively, build high-performing teams, and grow in their executive careers. I've seen executives thrive with great communication skills, and I've seen others struggle with communication challenges. In almost every engagement I've had, communication has been a key component for growth—whether it's the method, content, delivery, or timing.

As mentioned before, **verbal communication** has suffered as people rush through whatever they have to say with little thought or attention to the results. Effective verbal communication has three key components: clear message (content); clear delivery; and a listening, informed audience. The content of the messages must be understandable, relevant, and easily followed. The words used should be easily understood and the sequence of what is said should make sense. The message should be clear and concise with enough specifics to be understood but not so many as to be confusing.

I have worked with executives who struggle with either end of being wordy in their communication. Some executives use as few words as possible so their messages become almost cryptic. Their audience often leaves having to fill in the blanks, make assumptions, guess, or just plain stalls not knowing what to do. I have seen additional meetings scheduled once an executive has left so participants can try to decipher as a group the intended message. Needless to say, lacking enough clarity and information can lead to errors in interpretation, significant inefficiencies, and a frustrated workforce.

Conversely, I have seen executives use too many words or say too much with the same outcome—confusion and inefficiencies. I worked with one executive who spoke with his stream of consciousness, basically thinking aloud and taking his audience on long journeys through his thought process and down many different paths—losing the audience along the way. He's an incredibly smart leader but his challenges in communicating make it difficult for others to follow him.

How can communication be made more clear and concise? When

possible, prepare for conversations ahead of time—particularly if the subject is complicated, sensitive, or particularly important. Think about the key points that need to be made, the details (if any) that need to be provided, and any required background. At first, writing these down may help until it becomes second nature and can be done in your head. Then put the key points in a sequence that makes it easier for the audience to understand. Question yourself about the level of detail and depth of the background story required to make sure these are needed for the audience and to prevent yourself from being too wordy. If necessary, practice what you want to say beforehand. Even if the conversation doesn't go as planned, you'll be able to draw from some of the phrases you've come up with and will have determined ahead of time the level of detail you need to provide.

When answering a question, give yourself a few seconds to respond so you can think about what you want to say. If it's a more complicated answer, ask for time to think or offer to get back with an answer by a specific time so you can give yourself the needed time to think. If you're ready to answer the question, try doing so in two statements or less to prevent saying too much or going into tangents or unwanted stories. Rather than answering with a story or background, start with the answer and provide more only if needed or requested by the audience. You might start with "Yes (or no) because ... (in one or two sentences)." Then you can ask your audience if your answer was clear, actually answered their question, or if they would like more information such as the background or your thought process.

Be aware of the language used when communicating verbally (and in writing). Using the word *I* can signify ownership or taking credit, which is appropriate if you're talking about your opinion or something just related to you. If others are involved, using *I* can sound self-serving or inappropriate. When using *I* to discuss a problem, unless you're taking responsibility, chances are you're sounding defensive. Using the word *we* can connote sharing and sound team-oriented. It can also be sharing the blame if used to discuss a problem. Use of the word *you* can appear blaming or confrontational when discussing how a problem or issue occurred.

The delivery of verbal messages can significantly influence how the messages are received. The tone used in messages can signify the importance, seriousness, and emotions behind a message. The tone provides information about the messages and lets the audience know if the speaker is kidding, angry, confrontational, or passive. The tone used can completely change the meaning of the messages received by the audience. A potentially benign statement made with an angry or accusatory tone can send a completely different message than the same statement made with a soft, even tone. It's very common to have misunderstandings due to the perceived tones in messages. Be aware of the tone used and potential translations by the audience to help keep your messages clear.

The volume used for verbal communication can impact how well messages are received and can also lead to perceptions made by the audience about the speakers. This can be difficult for people with naturally soft voices. I have worked with clients who received feedback in their 360 Assessments about their soft voices and how it impacts their executive presence (discussed further in chapter 9). My clients' soft voices opened up opportunities for others to talk over them and, in some cases, take over their meetings. The participants providing the feedback also noted that the soft voices unfortunately created perceptions of a lack of confidence and weak leadership of the clients. Increasing the volume of speech for these clients helped them have a more confident and authoritative presence.

Conversely, loud volumes can overwhelm or intimidate the audience and prevent them from participating in discussions and presenting thoughts, ideas, opinions, or questions. This can have a detrimental impact as well. Leaders with loud, boisterous voices may have to make extra efforts to get others to participate in discussions and provide opinions.

The overuse of fillers in verbal communication can also impact the perceptions others have of the leaders. Fillers are the *uh's* and *um's* often used while the speaker is thinking—or saying them can just be a habit, nervous or otherwise. The use of fillers can give the impression of nervousness or lack of confidence in the speaker. Preparing for conversations or speeches in advance and practicing in everyday conversations can significantly reduce the frequency of fillers.

When verbally communicating to others—whether in conversation, meetings, or presentations—the ability to read the audience and adjust to it can significantly improve the effectiveness of the communication. Preparing ahead of time with consideration for who the audience is will allow you to start with an effective approach. This is particularly the case in one-on-one meetings or smaller groups—as there are fewer people to focus on, read, and adjust to. It is important to communicate with different people differently based on their preferences in how they give and receive information. Some people prefer a more formal, direct, informative approach with focus on the data and facts. Others prefer a more casual, social approach with focus on the relationships. Some like a lot of details; others prefer the highlights. Reading and adjusting to the preferred style of your audience will improve your ability to be heard and understood.

When addressing larger groups, your ability to read the room will allow you to make adjustments to your audience as needed. You can do this by reading the body language and facial expressions for understanding and acceptance of what is being said and if you're speaking at the appropriate pace. If the audience is making good eye contact with expected facial expressions that respond to what you're saying, indications are favorable that you are reaching them. If the audience is distracted, avoiding eye contact (or have glazed eyes), or are looking at their watches or handheld devices, you may be losing them. As you read the room, adjust your content, tone, or pace as appropriate to make your communication as effective as possible.

Nonverbal communication can also have a significant impact on how messages are received and can make statements with nothing even being said. Have you ever seen someone walking with a slumped posture, eyes to the ground, and a frown on their face? You can tell that person is having a tough time with something or is upset—even though they haven't said a word.

Nonverbal communication includes facial expressions, eye contact, body posture, and gestures. Some nonverbal communication is more obvious, such as rolling of the eyes, facial expressions, and gestures. Others are more subtle, such as eye contact and posture. All can provide added information to any verbal messages that are given and received.

Some of my clients have had challenges with nonverbal communication. Their body language negatively impacted the perceptions others had of them. When some clients got upset, angry, or frustrated, their necks turned red, their body posture changed (either more upright and forward or sitting back with arms crossed), and their speech patterns changed (speaking faster and louder). Their audiences interpreted these nonverbal cues as aggressive or defensive. When other clients got nervous their necks turned red, body posture changed (more slumped and closed in), and speech patterns became slower and softer. Their audiences interpreted these nonverbal cues as reflecting insecurity or a lack of confidence. In all cases, the clients' nonverbal communication hurts the perceptions others had of them and their leadership abilities.

Nonverbal communication can be managed by becoming aware of what our natural nonverbal cues are, preparing for situations that can trigger them, and practicing to prevent them from occurring. Chapter 9 provides added tools for managing emotions that can come through in nonverbal communication.

Something that often and unfortunately can get worse over time for executives—but is just as important the higher they climb—is **listening skills**. Executives can lose focus because they're rushed for time, have heard it all before, just want to get to the bottom line, or think they know the answers already. They do this by finishing others' sentences, quickly and consistently nodding as if to say, "I get it, move on," flipping to the back of the presentation, taking over the conversation, looking at their computer or Blackberry, or just zoning out.

In general, there are far too many people talking and not enough listening. People want to be heard but are not willing or disciplined to listen. The skill of listening is grossly underused and has, therefore, become weak—like a muscle that hasn't been exercised in a while.

Most of us don't intend to be poor listeners or ignore others; we're just trying to do so much at once and make sure we're heard that our listening skills suffer. Test your listening skills this way: count how many times you multitask when listening to others (in person or on the phone), and count how much time you spend speaking versus asking other people questions and listening.

There is much to be gained by actively listening to others. Active listening involves responding to the person speaking either with comments or questions, or non-verbally with nods or other vocalizations (*mm hm*) that let the speaker know you are listening, understand, agree, or disagree. Passive listening has no response and gives the speaker no indication that he or she has been heard or understood. Actively listening with good questions provides a lot of opportunity to gather valuable information and learn new things. The more questions you ask, the more opportunities you have to learn. Active listening also helps build relationships by showing that you care what others have to say. People want to be heard, not just listened to.

Listening skills can be improved by first removing any and all distractions. Don't look at the computer or any handheld devices while others are talking to you. If you are in your office, move away from your computer or minimize any open computer windows that could distract you. Email is often the biggest distraction on the computer. I encourage my clients to turn off the chime that indicates new messages have arrived to remove that distraction. If you are leaving your office for a meeting, try leaving your handheld device(s) behind. Few of us are in positions that require immediate access and those that are typically have assistants who can reach them for urgent matters.

Maintaining eye contact will help you focus on what is being said and will reassure the speaker that you are listening. It can be quite frustrating for a speaker trying to talk to someone whose attention is focused elsewhere. It leaves the speaker feeling as if what he or she has to say isn't important. It's not only rude on the part of the listener but also impacts his or her ability to hear and absorb what is being said. If you're making excuses for why you can be distracted in a meeting such as, "I don't need to hear this part," or "This meeting is a waste of my time," then I would ask: *Why are you wasting your time in that meeting?* Or, *What can you do to make the meeting more productive?*

If you find that your mind has wandered during a conversation, apologize to the speaker, let him or her know that you lost focus for a minute, and then ask the person to repeat what was said. This will ensure that you didn't miss anything important, illustrate to the speaker that you want to hear what he or she has to say, and show the speaker how to do this himself or herself when needed. Summarize your key takeaways to make sure you've synthesized the information or message the speaker intended.

While in a meeting, focus your attention on the speaker and what's being said. If you lose it, bring it back as soon as you realize it. If needed, play back what you've heard in your own words to show that you are listening and to confirm that what you heard was what the speaker intended. Engage more in the discussion by asking deeper open-ended questions to help further the thinking of all participants in the meeting.

Executives should practice active listening skills in every conversation and meeting. After all, the higher an executive climbs, the more time is spent listening to others. Executives typically aren't close enough to the details of the business to know everything and, therefore, rely on the information the organization provides. Given that, it is important for executives to ask questions while actively listening, not only to gather information, but also to help the organization think at a deeper level. One of the most powerful skills an executive can have is the ability to ask the right questions at the right time. These powerful questions can help identify issues and opportunities and help further the thinking of everyone in the room. At their levels, executives typically bring a breadth of experiences, strategic insights, and broad views that can help their organizations focused on the details to think about the bigger picture. One practice some executives find useful is to jot down key points or questions as others are presenting or just talking, then ask open-ended questions that probe deeper—not with aggression, but with a desire to learn more. Examples of how some of these questions might start with are:

"What are the risks/opportunities of _____?"
"How has ____ worked before?"
"What would happen if we were to _____?"
"How can we approach _____ differently?"

The time spent actively listening at the expense of multitasking may feel inefficient, but it will pay off in the long run with clearer communication, fewer misunderstandings, and less redundant conversations and meetings. Active listening also fosters connecting with people and understanding them more comprehensively.

Poor listening skills are one of the more common complaints I hear in executives' 360 Assessments. Everyone wants to be heard, and you should want to hear what people have to say. Demonstrate that you have been listening so they know they have been heard.

Now more than ever, **written communication** are being relied on as a preferred method of communicating. This is particularly the case with emails and texting. Today's technology makes written communication so easy and fast, but the downsides and risks can be significant. These include:

- People avoid important face-to-face discussions.
- People are more direct than they would be face-to-face.
- People are more careless about what is written so messages are unclear or misunderstood.
- Messages are void of tone so readers inject their own based on their frame of reference.
- Written communication does not promote a dialogue.
- A writer cannot read body language or see the reactions of the audience to adjust the message or delivery immediately.
- Written communication provides fewer opportunities to brainstorm and share ideas.
- Sensitive and/or confidential information can easily end up in the wrong hands.
- Sarcasm or jokes can be misunderstood.
- Messages become a permanent record.

- People quickly and carelessly transfer ownership of tasks.

I have seen executives get into trouble with the inappropriate use of email. The results have included demotions, loss of jobs, legal action, and significant damage to reputations and careers. Email has become so easy and convenient to use in the office or on the road that the potential ramifications are often overlooked. Some use email to say something they wouldn't say in person. Some use it just to get something they have to deal with off their plates. Others use email to make a statement without having to hear the response. Ultimately, email is a one-way conversation.

Keeping in mind that emails are considered legal documents and are never completely deleted or destroyed, there is a liability that can come with using email. Delicate, sensitive, and propriety information shared on email can be easily shared with the wrong people or get in the wrong or unintended hands. Information that can lead to legal action, information about competitive advantages, or personal information about others—are all dangerous topics to address in email. I have seen executives send sexually explicit and obviously inappropriate emails to employees. What an incredibly risky thing to do!

While the above are more obvious misuses of email, there are more subtle misuses of email. All too often I see managers try to manage their people over email. They delegate work on email rather than walk across the hall and have a productive discussion about it. They provide feedback on email, which can be perceived as an insensitive and cowardly way to provide it. They discuss sensitive topics or try to resolve conflict on email rather than in person. I have seen significant repercussions for managers using email to discuss controversial or sensitive topics.

Another risk to keep in mind when using email is that the reader assumes the tone used by the writer. Conflict often occurs because the tone received is not the tone intended. Using sarcasm, jokes, or *just kidding* in emails can be misinterpreted—and by the time you try to explain the real intent, the damage has been done.

Emails are drastically overused. They should only be used to share objective, non-sensitive, non-controversial information that does not require a discussion. Examples include: "We will meet at *x* time and *x* place"; "The number you are looking for is *x*" (assuming it's not sensitive or controversial); "The name of the person you want to contact is *x*"; or "We will not have a meeting today." Email should be the last resort for any lengthy discussion. In-person is the preferred method for anything sensitive, controversial, delicate, or requiring a discussion. The phone is the second preferred method. See exhibit 7-a for a decision tree on communication methods to use.

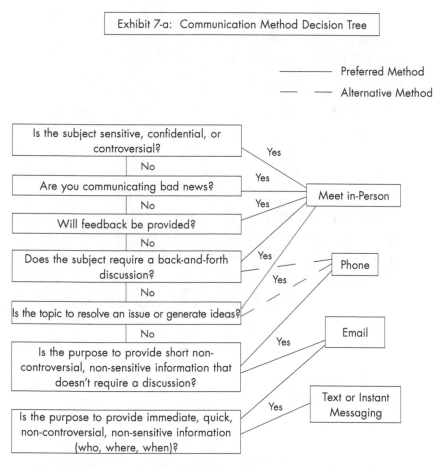

Exhibit 7-a: Communication Method Decision Tree

Today's global economy with offices and employees located all over the world can make it difficult to have in-person discussions for difficult or sensitive topics, in which case the phone may be the best option. Again, email should be avoided for any sensitive or confidential information or to provide feedback. If email is the only option for communicating potentially controversial information due to timing and/or logistical complications, consider these tips to reduce the risk of unexpected negative reactions to what is written.

- Add recipients' addresses just before sending to prevent accidentally hitting *send* before it has been reviewed.
- Sleep on it if you are emotional about the topic or response to give yourself time to calm down.
- Have someone else review it for clear content, sensitivities, and possible tone misunderstandings.
- Make sure email is the only option.

All executives and leaders should have a Communication Plan—either formal or informal—to help determine what ongoing and occasional communication and meetings are necessary. A communication plan outlines how, when, and with whom ongoing communication (via meetings or otherwise) are going to occur. The purpose of this communication might be to inform, be visible to the organization, demonstrate leadership, provide updates, and/or share successes. Without a specific plan, these important opportunities often get forgotten. Lack of communication is another common piece of feedback I hear in many executives' 360 Assessments. Exhibit 8-2 is an example of a communication plan.

Exhibit 8-2: Communication Plan			
Audience	Purpose	Method	Frequency
Direct Reports	Stay informed, gather updates, provide support	20-minute meetings (in-person for local, via phone for other locations)	Weekly

Exhibit 8-2: Communication Plan			
<u>Audience</u>	<u>Purpose</u>	<u>Method</u>	<u>Frequency</u>
Direct Reports	Share information, resolve organizational issues, discuss new risks and opportunities	1-hour meetings (conference in other locations)	Monthly
Entire Organization	Find new opportunities, share knowledge and insights	Blog	Weekly
Entire Organization	Be visible and supportive, share information and insights	Walk the halls for 30 minutes	Weekly
Entire Organization	Share information, provide business updates, recognize accomplish-ments	Email Newsletter	Monthly
Entire Organization	Share updates and information, have guest speakers	Company Meeting	Biannually

Many executives are nervous about communication plans for fear of not knowing what to say, boring people, not being productive, or being overexposed. That is why I suggest getting feedback and ideas on the communication plans. Ask your direct reports and others what the organization wants to hear, how often, and by what method (meetings, emails, blogs, and so forth.). Periodically ask for feedback again and tweak the plan as needed.

Summary

Executives can grow by improving communication skills because they will effectively hear what is being said to them, clearly articulate the messages they wish to convey, and ask the right questions to uncover issues and opportunities. All of these will help executives stay informed, make the right decisions, and keep their organizations on the right track.

Companies can grow when executive communication is clear, concise, and appropriately delivered. As information is effectively shared and heard, risks are mitigated, opportunities are uncovered, employees are motivated, and the right decisions are made.

CHAPTER 8:

....

Efficient & Effective Meetings

I do not go to a meeting merely to give my own ideas. If that were all, I might write my fellow members a letter. But neither do I go simply to learn other people's ideas. If that were all, I might ask each to write me a letter. I go to a meeting in order that all together we may create a group idea, an idea which will be better than all of our ideas added together. For this group idea will not be produced by any process of addition, but by the interpenetration of us all.

—Mary Parker Follett

A common complaint, not just with executives but also across organizations, is the number of inefficient, ineffective, time-wasting meetings. They hurt the individual employee's productivity, and if you multiply that by the number of people in each meeting every day, that's a significant productivity issue for any company. Meetings are so easy to schedule—especially now with calendar technology—that all anyone has to do is invite people and find a place to meet.

Meetings are a necessary and important part of doing business, no doubt. But often, little thought is given to how to keep the meetings productive and efficient. Proactively taking the time to ensure each meeting provides value is well worth the effort, and it can have a significant impact on a company's bottom-line as well as on employee morale—and it's not difficult to do.

There are six components to efficient and effective meetings: the purpose, agenda, participants, time, facilitation, and conclusion with next steps. Giving some thought to each of these when scheduling every meeting can have a significantly positive impact on the effectiveness of every meeting.

The trigger to scheduling a meeting is typically some kind of **purpose**. Something might need to be communicated, coordinated, or addressed so a meeting is scheduled. As discussed in the previous chapter, some topics should be addressed face-to-face in meetings, and some can be written and sent in various forms (email, text). Careful consideration should be given to the purpose to determine whether or not a meeting actually needs to be held and how to plan for each of the next five components.

The following reasons are generally appropriate for having a meeting:

- **The topic is confidential, sensitive, or controversial**.
- **Bad news is being communicated**.
- **Significant issues are being resolved**.
- **Ideas are being generated and discussed**.
- **Feedback is being given**.
- **Relationships are being forged**.
- Activities are being coordinated.
- Direction needs to be given to more than two or three people with the opportunity to answer questions that all participants can benefit from hearing.
- Questions or concerns could be raised that others need to hear.
- Unfiltered facts are needed.
- A topic requires discussion with more than two or three people.

Meetings can be held in person, on the phone, and nowadays on video. There are some obvious benefits and drawbacks to each.

Meetings held in person promote idea generation and exchange; allow for participants to read each other's body language; help ensure everyone is paying attention; and promote building relationships. The drawback to in-person meetings is that it takes more time and coordination to get everyone in the same room. Meetings via phone can be easier to coordinate and take less time, but they don't offer the benefits of in-person meetings. In the list above, the top six reasons for having meetings warrant—and should require—in-person meetings. The rest of the list can be handled over the phone depending on the seriousness and complexity of the topic and the ease of meeting in person versus over the phone. Video conferencing is being adopted in many industries but there still appears to be a reluctance to use it—possibly because of the discomfort some feel about being on video. Time will tell if it becomes a more popular use for business as people get more used to it in their personal lives using services such as Skype.

When thinking through the purpose of a meeting, ask yourself these questions to help you determine if a meeting is necessary, to help you prepare for a productive meeting, and to ensure the outcome is what you want and expect: *What answers or actions should be determined in the meeting? What information do I need to leave behind in the meeting? What questions do I need answered in the meeting? What impressions do I need to leave on the participants of the meeting (urgency, leadership, and so on)? What could derail the meeting?* A purpose that is clearly thought through and communicated can set up a meeting for success as the participants will have clarity about what the expectations are and understand what results (decisions, deliverables or actions) are expected at the end.

Unfortunately, there are other less desirable and less productive reasons people hold meetings that are often frustrating for the participants. These include:

- To revisit a topic previously discussed in another meeting
- To prepare for meetings scheduled for the purpose of preparing for more meetings scheduled in the future
- To provide redundant updates on business that hasn't changed

- To let the participants know that whatever was to originally be reviewed at the meeting is not ready for review

Often in large corporations pre-meetings are held in preparation for other meetings. This practice can be incredibly time-consuming and unproductive for those preparing for all of these meetings. If pre-meetings are necessary to prepare an executive for another meeting, try to consolidate all of the pre-meetings into one or send out materials that can be reviewed without a formal meeting. If you are scheduling a meeting that falls into one of the topics above, consider the outcome you expect and make sure it's worth the time spent by all of the participants, including yourself.

A clearly defined purpose will help build an effective agenda. An **agenda** is a more detailed plan of what will be discussed and how a meeting will flow. Agendas can be very specific with each topic and a timeline, and sent out to participants in advance. They can also be less formal—jotted down on a piece of paper by the leader of the meeting for him or her to follow. The length of the meetings, complexity of the topics, and number of participants help determine how formal the agendas need to be. Ongoing weekly meetings may not need a formal agenda unless the topics change each week. Agendas can help large, long, complex meetings stay on track and ensure the desired results are achieved.

When creating agendas, whether they are formal or not, the following should be considered:

- Purpose previously defined
- Topics to be discussed
- Timeline (for longer or more complex meetings covering many topics)
- Information required ahead of time
- Any preparation required by participants
- Results, decisions, or deliverables expected at the end of the meeting
- Time for questions
- Recap of outcome and plan for next steps

There are many benefits to creating an agenda before each meeting. It helps prepare the leader to run the meeting efficiently and effectively. It will help him or her think about whom the participants need to be, what information or preparation is needed for the meeting, how the meeting should flow between topics, what could derail the meeting, and what the final outcome needs to be. If formal agendas are sent out prior to the meeting it helps prepare the attendees as well by ensuring any information or preparation required for the meeting is communicated, and making sure everyone knows what the expected outcome is. Even if a formal agenda is not needed, taking a few minutes before each meeting to think through the agenda can mean the difference between having an efficient and successful meeting or wasting a lot of time and money.

Once the purpose and agenda have been clearly defined, carefully consider who the **participants** need to be. There can be a tendency to invite too many people to cover all bases or out of fear of hurting someone's feelings. While they may seem like legitimate reasons, they may not be productive ones; those issues can be handled other ways. Conversely, some may not have enough people in a meeting, a problem that ends up creating more follow-up meetings. When creating the list of participants, think about who will be bringing critical information, who will need to take immediate *action* as a result of the meeting, who needs to participate in the decisions made in the meeting, and who will be *directly* impacted by decisions made in a meeting. When considering these criteria alone the list can be long; offset it by trying to invite the minimal number of participants and including only one from each department or organization impacted, if possible. Try to avoid including those who might just *want* to hear or know about what's discussed in the meeting, those who just want to be seen in a meeting, or those who are minimally impacted and don't need to be present for the entire meeting. They can be informed later in a more efficient manner. In the end, you want as few participants as needed, not as many as possible.

In some company cultures it seems most meetings take exactly one hour. Some are stretched longer than needed to make it to one hour. Some are rushed at the end to squeeze them within the hour. Others are ended without reaching the desired result and then continued later with yet another meeting. Estimating how long a meeting will take is tough, so most round it to the next hour. If we could shave fifteen minutes off of each meeting that didn't require that extra time, think about the time that would be saved for the individuals and resulting increased productivity for the company. Sticking to agendas can help meetings stay focused and end when the result is achieved versus when the clock strikes the hour. Some executives hold their regular daily or weekly update meetings with all participants standing up; this can help keep the meetings focused and short.

There are some behaviors that contribute to the inefficiencies of meetings. These include:

- Participants arriving late
- The leader or participants coming unprepared
- Participants distracted by handheld devices, laptops, or side conversations
- Lack of participation by attendees
- Discussions going off-topic
- Participants speaking to be heard versus adding value
- Participants repeating what others have said in efforts to be heard
- Participants talking over others
- Participants returning to previous discussions preventing the topics from moving forward

Leaders can and should help ensure that these unproductive behaviors are managed. First, leaders should be aware of when they themselves are guilty of any of these bad behaviors. If a leader is consistently late for meetings, chances are his employees are doing the same. This means every meeting has people waiting on others, which is an incredible waste of time and money. Leaders are encouraged to provide feedback and coach employees who exhibit these bad behaviors.

Active **facilitation** in each meeting can also help ensure it runs smoothly and effectively. The job of the facilitator is to kick off the meeting with the purpose, expectations, and deliverables of the meeting to make sure all participants are "on the same page." The facilitator then helps keep the discussion on topic and moving forward, makes sure attendees participate and are heard, and manages some of the bad behaviors mentioned above. Finally, the facilitator ends the meeting with a conclusion and next steps. Facilitation is a skill not taught in school, so it has to be self-taught or learned through training classes. A well-facilitated meeting can be amazingly impactful with participants leaving the meeting well-informed, feeling like they've contributed and been heard, and clear about their follow-up actions. The facilitator of a meeting is assumed to be the one who scheduled it (or the leader of the group) unless identified and communicated otherwise. It's important that every meeting have an active facilitator.

The final component to effective and efficient meetings is the **conclusion and next steps**. Every meeting should have a conclusion and next steps. This is important closure for summarizing and clarifying the decisions that were made, ensuring the participants know and buy-in to the decisions and next steps, and making sure the outcome of the meeting is followed up on. Meetings without conclusions and next steps leave participants unsure about the final decisions; they end up making assumptions about what the next steps are, who is responsible for them, and when they are expected to be completed. Tremendous inefficiencies can result with unclear expectations, duplicate efforts, late responses, or nothing getting done at all.

The conclusion should include a recap of the decisions that were made in the meeting. The next steps should be actions (with verbs) versus ideas or projects that can be interpreted differently. The actions should have designated owners of each and dates for when the actions—or at least updates on the actions—can be expected. Only one person should be designated per action. More than one can result in duplicate efforts, conflicting efforts, or nothing getting done at all. Even if the action requires more than one participant, only one should be designated as the leader or the one responsible for that action. The next steps should also include what the follow-up is to that meeting. Will there be a follow-up meeting to discuss progress or will other means be used for keeping the right people informed? When the participants leave the meetings there should be no question about what the decisions and outcomes were, and what the next steps are.

Even if you are a participant in a meeting and not leading or facilitating it, there are things you can do to make it as efficient and effective for yourself as possible. Take a few minutes before each meeting and ask yourself these questions:

1. *What role am I playing in this meeting? Leader? Supporter? Participator? Audience? Devil's Advocate?*
2. *What impressions do I want to leave behind? Empathetic? Strong leader? Supporter? Change agent? Collaborator? Good listener? Decision-maker?*
3. *What information do I need to obtain in this meeting?*
4. *What information do I need to provide?*

Then, at the end of the meeting think about how well you have achieved the answers to these questions and add any additional comments or ask questions as necessary and appropriate. Also, make sure you have a clear understanding of what you can expect from the outcome of the meeting and any follow ups expected of you (information, decisions, and so forth).

As we all try to juggle the meetings, priorities, and fire drills of each day by moving things around and removing the lowest priorities, the common casualties are the staff meetings and one-on-one update meetings with our staff, which often get moved or cancelled completely. Unfortunately, those are some of the most important meetings if done well. In my work as an executive coach I see an interesting dynamic. I see people complain about going to wasteful staff meetings, yet in executives' 360 Assessments employees ask for more time with their peers and bosses. The biggest complaint I hear about staff meetings is the time wasted listening to updates around the room that haven't changed since the previous meetings. This feedback is indicative of the need for more efficient and effective meetings with the staff.

It's important to communicate with your direct reports as a group or individually at least once a week. It doesn't have to be for a whole hour or even a half hour, and it doesn't have to be in person (unless the topic warrants it). You can touch base with each direct report via phone for fifteen to twenty minutes a week. I have encouraged many clients to adopt this practice and they have realized a return on this time investment. They are kept better informed, have proactively learned about risks and opportunities they can act on or coach around, and they have more trust in—and improved relationships with— their direct reports. Their direct reports meet more expectations that are consistently clarified and reinforced, receive more direction and coaching as needed, feel more supported by their bosses, and feel more connected to the organization.

Staff meetings are good for organizations that need to coordinate work or could benefit from hearing the updates or challenges from the others in the group because of potential impacts or learning opportunities. If members of a staff don't need to coordinate work on a weekly basis or hear updates from the others, a monthly staff meeting might make more sense as long as weekly one-on-ones are still happening.

Staff meetings or one-on-ones with direct reports provide the following opportunities:

- To reinforce expectations
- To uncover and discuss risks and opportunities
- To share information (up, down, and across)
- To coach and develop leadership skills
- To build relationships

Whether you have one-on-ones with your direct reports or staff meetings, there are things you can do to keep the meetings productive and worth the effort. Keep them short. Try to avoid redundant updates and keep them to less than an hour for weekly staff meetings and less than half an hour for weekly one-on-ones. Ask good open-ended questions to uncover the risks and opportunities to be focused on. Exhibit 8-a has some sample questions. Use agendas for staff meetings if specific topics that change frequently are going to be discussed or if preparation is required by the staff. Get feedback from your direct reports on what they would like to discuss at staff meetings or in one-on-ones. Finally, try to avoid cancelling or consistently rescheduling staff meetings, particularly one-on-ones. These meetings should have a higher level of priority. Based on 360 Assessments I received for executives, consistently cancelling or rescheduling these meetings sends a message to your direct report that they and what they are working on are not important. It also frustrates the direct reports who might have topics they need to cover or issues to discuss at these meetings. Lastly, it indirectly gives permission to the direct reports to do the same thing to their direct reports and thus cancelling these important meetings becomes part of the culture.

Exhibit 8-a: Sample Questions for Direct Reports

- What went well this week?
- What are your biggest challenges this week?
- What are the top three opportunities you're chasing?
- What are your top concerns right now?
- What's keeping you up at night?
- What's not getting done or making the progress you had hoped for or anticipated?
- What can I do to help you?
- What do you need from me?

Summary

<u>Executives</u> can grow by holding efficient and effective meetings because they will be more proactively and better informed to make decisions, set direction, or course correct. They will be more productive with less time wasted in ineffective meetings. They will have more opportunity to coach and develop their direct reports. Their teams will be more productive and have a higher morale.

<u>Companies</u> can grow with efficient and effective meetings as information is more readily disseminated, and risks and opportunities are more proactively discovered and acted upon. Time and money is saved by not holding inefficient or ineffective meetings. Employees are more productive and motivated, reducing turnover and saving the company money. The culture will be positively influenced with better focus and more opportunities for coaching and development.

CHAPTER 9:

• •

Executive Presence

The challenge of leadership is to be strong, but not rude; be kind, but not weak; be bold, but not bully; be thoughtful, but not lazy; be humble, but not timid; be proud, but not arrogant; have humor, but without folly.

—*Jim Rohn*

I n leadership, the hardest thing to define and describe is *executive presence.* That's the term used to identify the persona, characteristics, tone, attitude, confidence, impressions, and so forth that makes an executive look and act like one. It's hard to identify and describe because it's really in the eye of the beholder. Words used to describe it include confident, calm, decisive, professional, focused, commanding, intelligent, influential, motivating, inspiring, charismatic, powerful, having natural leadership ability, courageous, sophisticated, having a certain *je ne sais quoi*, possessing bravado. I'm a big believer in the idea that leaders earn that distinction from those they lead, not from a title or level of responsibilities. That said, aside from the expected attributes of a leader or executive—such as contributions made, expertise in their given field, education, and experience—there's also expected conduct.

Don't underestimate the value and importance of having executive presence. A lack of executive presence or a weak one can prevent an executive from getting to the next level. Executive presence is needed internally to gain the respect at all levels of the company, including the owners and/or the board. It's needed externally to gain the respect of Wall Street, analysts, and customers. Even those rare executives who have made it to the top for specific talents—like Bill Gates and Steve Jobs—have had to learn behaviors required of their roles. You can see over time how their behaviors changed and became more polished and respectable.

I am often asked in my coaching practice to help executives develop their executive presence. This is often the final piece of the puzzle required to promote someone to the top levels. Some believe you either have it or you don't, and that it's something you are born with. It is true that there are many leaders born with natural charisma, a commanding personality, and leadership appeal—though even those individuals can have other shortcomings in executive presence, like integrity or discretion. Those who weren't born with some of these characteristics can still develop behaviors that build on their executive presence. It doesn't require changing who we are or changing our individual personalities. It requires modifying and practicing behaviors expected of executives.

Emotions

Executives are expected to make decisions in the best interest of the company based on information and input, not based on *emotions*. This isn't easy to do. Often, executives have to fire or lay off people they like, kill projects or sell off divisions they feel emotionally vested in. When, how, and how often emotions are used by executives can have a profound impact on their reputations, effectiveness, and even careers. I have been asked on many occasions to coach executives on their emotional reactions because their emotions were getting in the way of their career advancement. Emotions are appropriate at the workplace when showing or expressing empathy in difficult situations—like layoffs or deaths. Expressing emotions like sadness, despair, fear, and anger about a business issue may not be seen as appropriate.

The emotions an executive expresses can have a deep impact on an organization because it provides a gauge about the health of the organization. So, if an executive facing difficult situations expresses fear, sadness, or anger, the organization may start to have doubts about the health of the organization or effectiveness of its leader. Employees can lose faith in the organization and/or the leader. People in the organization count on their leader to lead them through difficult times. They want to know the leader is in control of the situation and handling it calmly, effectively, and confidently. The executive's reactions can cause similar reactions within the organization, which can then lead to fear, defeatism, poor morale, and employee turnover.

Executives' emotional reactions, particularly anger, can have a profound impact on their direct reports. Negative emotions like anger can certainly lead to poor morale as they put an air of negativity in the environment. Working with emotional executives can be like walking on eggshells, as those around them are afraid to say anything that could set the executives off. Direct reports can become fearful of presenting any issues or challenges. If the direct reports become fearful of presenting any bad news, they may start withholding or hiding the information and that can be dangerous to the executives and the companies. It certainly doesn't help promote the open communication that is critical to any executive. Finally, it can prompt direct reports to behave the same way with their teams, as it becomes assumed that this is acceptable and possibly even expected behavior.

Keep in mind that expressed emotions are not only verbal. Often, it's the *non-verbal* emotional reactions that give away the emotional state of an executive. Such non-verbal reactions include turning red in the face, frowning, breaking eye contact, fixing eye contact on a particular person, sitting back in the chair, and crossing the arms. I would offer that non-verbal communication can be even more attention-getting than verbal communication. It gives people something to focus on, talk about, interpret, and guess about what's bothering the executive— versus knowing it with verbal communication.

If you think getting angry and yelling makes you look tough, don't kid yourself. It's more likely to make you look weak (like you can't handle the circumstances), threatened, defensive, out of control, or like a bully. Anger and frustration are often overused emotions in the workplace. This overuse can lose the effectiveness of the emotion. It becomes a *cry wolf* scenario, so when the executive is really angry it's given the same attention as when the executive reacts to more minor issues. It can also give the perception of the executive being defensive. The executive may appear to get angry because others disagree with or challenge him or her, or offer other opinions or ideas. This makes the issue all about the executive and his or her ego versus being about the business. The executive now looks insecure to others. If an executive was just surprised to learn (without previous knowledge or warning) that the organization was going to miss its numbers by 50 percent, that's a good reason to get angry. An executive who expresses anger often—because others disagree with him or her or offer other ideas—is overusing the emotion and could be held back career-wise because of it.

In most cases, executives who become emotional often do so because they feel threatened, attacked, or insulted. The emotion becomes a defensive reaction. This is usually indicative of taking things too personally. If someone disagrees with them, they become agitated, angry, or defensive. If someone comes up with a better idea, they become threatened. If business is not doing well, they are afraid it will make them look bad. This is not easy for an executive to admit to, so if you tend to be emotional on a regular basis, challenge yourself to think about the underlying cause of these emotions. Once you become aware of the thoughts behind the emotions, you can focus on changing the behavior. It comes from inside. By de-personalizing work, you can approach it with objectivity and focus on the right solutions—versus those that will make you look good. It's an interesting paradox. The more emotional and defensive someone gets trying to protect his or her self-esteem, the more apparent it is and the worse the person looks. By consistently and objectively focusing on the best business solutions all the time, the individual will find the best results and achieve them with an air of confidence because they're not taking things personally or reacting defensively. Exhibit 9-a provides tips for managing emotions.

Exhibit 9-a: Tips for Managing Emotions
- Be prepared before meetings and think about your reactions to any potential hot buttons for you.
- Think about the impression you want to make.
- Take deep breaths and pause before responding.
- Give yourself enough time to think before responding. If a topic is particularly upsetting to you, explain that you need time to think about it and schedule a follow up.
- Keep reminding yourself that this is not about you. It's about the company.

Even under the worst of circumstances, the more you can control your composure and respond objectively, the more confident and better you'll look—and the more you will be respected for it. Save your emotional responses for strategic moments when you need to make an important point or add emphasis. This shouldn't be happening more than four times a year or the effect will be diminished.

For many of us, our professional lives are such a big part of who we are. Our careers are part of our identities. We put a lot of ourselves into our careers. That's why it can be challenging to control our emotions because we feel so passionately about our jobs and, in some cases, our companies. Not only is it important to manage our emotions, it's also critical to manage the decisions that can come from feelings or emotions— whether those feelings are displayed or hidden, too. On several occasions I have seen executives make decisions to prevent embarrassing themselves, even when it wasn't the right decision to make. They may have overpromised something, made claims that weren't true, or are trying to cover up mistakes or performance issues. Most executives will face decisions at some point in their career that will force them to weigh *looking good* versus *doing the right thing*.

Priorities

One of the most difficult things an executive has to manage from a holistic standpoint is *priorities*. We are taught in business school that the number one priority as an employee and executive is to increase shareholder (or stakeholder) value. In the day-to-day world of tasks, meetings, projects, and objectives, it's easy to lose sight of that. It's only human to want to make decisions that may further our careers without thinking about how it impacts the organization. The decisions we make should be based on the following priorities: 1) What's in the best interest of the company? 2) What's in the best interest of the organization (division or department)? and 3) What's in the best interest of the individual, whether oneself or someone else? It is not uncommon for executives to have to make decisions for the benefit of their companies—but detrimental to themselves or their departments. For example, an executive may realize it's in the best interest of the company to outsource his or her particular area, which will mean the dismantling of the department and loss of his or her job. Even if the decision you make forces you to look for something new, it's a great selling point for the next opportunity. The fact that you did the right thing for the company at the expense of your self-interest is appealing and respectable. Chances are if you don't make the decision now on this opportunity that could land you out of a job, someone else will later. Take the bull by the horns, take control of the situation, and lead it yourself before it's imposed on you. The end result may be the same—you're out of a job—but you'll gain respect, control, and possibly better job opportunities.

If all leaders made company agendas a priority over individual, departmental, or divisional agendas, it could break down all the silos that plague so many companies. Think about how that could impact a company's ability to be efficient, implement change, foster the development of new ideas, and react to new market products, processes and conditions.

Integrity

Another powerful trait in successful leaders is *integrity*. It is also a fragile trait because one mistake or misunderstanding can jeopardize the perceived integrity an executive has forever. Employees want to work for and follow leaders they trust. They trust their leaders to be honest even with bad news, to make quick decisions based on as many facts as possible, to treat everyone fairly and equitably, and to support them constantly.

Integrity means admitting when you're wrong, or when you don't know or have an answer. When executives try to cover errors or make excuses, it's often obvious to others and they quickly lose the respect of their employees, peers, and bosses. Even worse is to cast the blame onto someone else. If you or a member of your team makes a mistake, you have to admit it and own it.

Having integrity means never lying. This can be challenging when an employee asks if you know something but you can't share it. Rather than lying by saying you don't know, you're better off admitting that you do but are not able to discuss it right then. If you lie and say you don't know and the employee finds out you knew it all along, that person may never trust what you say again.

Leaders with integrity are not afraid to stand up for what they believe—even if it's not popular with the organization and/or bosses. In the end they may not get their way, but they make sure they are heard and considered.

Early in my career, I worked for someone who made such an impression on me not only for his leadership but specifically for his integrity. This executive stood up for what he believed was right when faced with incredible pressure from his bosses. It was a risky position to take because he didn't follow along with his peers and just agree with something they didn't believe in against their better judgment. He let the top executives know he didn't agree with a course of action and why. It paid off because he earned the respect of his bosses and his employees, and it illustrated his level of integrity. I often think of him when facing tough issues. I ask myself: *What would Jim do in this situation?* Now that's impactful leadership!

Humility

One of the most respected, powerful, and recognized traits of successful executives is *humility*, particularly noted by those who work for the leader. People want to work for leaders who are effective but also humble. It gives the impression that the executives have the company's best interest in mind, and not their personal ego. It's not about them. It's about making the right decisions. *Confident but humble* is a tricky balance. The confidence should be about the decisions the executive makes. The humility is about the executive as a person. People want to work for leaders who have confidence in what they are doing versus being cocky about who they are. What behaviors give executives a perceived humility? Some examples include:

- Not being afraid to admit when they're wrong.
- Recognizing they may not be the smartest person in the room about particular topics.
- Not being afraid to own and take responsibility for things that go wrong under their leadership (then dealing with it internally).
- Not making decisions based on how they will look, or how it serves their best interest.
- Not being afraid to laugh at themselves and their shortcomings.
- Giving credit to their people versus taking it themselves.

People want to feel like they're working for something bigger than the career and success of an individual leader. Humble executives take the spotlight off themselves and keep it on the greater good of their organizations or companies as a whole.

It's easy to see how executives can lose perspective and focus too much on their individual desires, decisions that benefit them, and the illusion that they are always right. As they've climbed the ladder of success many have been surrounded by others who kiss up to them, wait on them, compliment them, agree with them, and always do what they ask. Their egos can easily get out of control. This is evident by the many executives who made poor decisions or judgments because they felt untouchable and their behaviors sometimes caught up to them in public ways. A recent example is the CEO of HP and the sexual harassment scandal. Don't be one of those executives who let their perceived power and authority go to their heads.

Executives also display humility when they share their successes with others. When executives give credit for accomplishments to those who participated and contributed to the successes, they share the spotlight and acknowledge the contributions made by others. Conversely, executives who take the credit either directly or indirectly (by not acknowledging the support of others) hurt their own credibility and perceptions of them. Most of what executives do requires the work, support, and participation of others. When they neglect to share the credit and successes, it is often obvious to others that they are keeping it for themselves.

Discretion

I continue to be amazed at the number of executives who don't manage sensitive information well. Whether it's personnel issues, organizational changes, personal issues about employees, highly confidential information, or even rumors, this information often starts with and is leaked by the executives at the top and middle. Aside from being the right thing to do, being *discreet* about sensitive information is important for executive presence. How much do you think employees' perceptions are impacted by executives who have loose lips or—worse yet—who contribute to the spreading of rumors?

Lack of discretion can also have a negative impact on business. Leaked competitive information can get to the competitors. Leaked personnel issues can embarrass employees or hurt their reputations, and can also put the company at risk for lawsuits. Leaked organizational changes can lead to premature decisions such as some leaving the company because they don't have all the information about the changes coming. Leaking personal issues is just plain wrong. Rumors are damaging and frustrating enough and they can have a significant impact on companies. An executive's role should be more about helping to stop or at least ignore rumors; the executive should be a role model for others to follow. As an executive you're being counted on and are responsible for being sensitive about information that is shared. When in doubt, keep your mouth shut. You can always share relevant business information later if and when it's appropriate, but once you let it out, you can't get it back.

I recently coached an executive for one of the top entertainment companies. His boss had told him about a fellow executive who was leaving the company and asked him to keep this information highly confidential. The circumstances around the reason the executive was leaving could have had legal ramifications. He told a few of his peers, then asked my opinion about whether or not that was appropriate. My thoughts are that if his boss wanted those others to know about it he would have told them himself. His boss also did not say to keep it confidential except for these few people. If you feel it's appropriate or necessary to share confidential information your boss has shared with you, check with him or her first. When it doubt, don't share confidential information.

Professionalism

Executives are expected to be professional anytime and every time they are with employees, customers, peers, and bosses—whether it's a business or casual function. This does not mean you can't dress down and have fun, but it *does* mean you have to be thoughtful about what you say and/or do. We've all seen employees and even executives drink too much at business parties and get talked about the next day. Some let their guards down and share confidential or inappropriate information.

Professionalism means behaving in a business-appropriate way. There is an even higher standard expected of executives. The standard of conduct expected of everyone in the workplace includes the following: moral and ethical obligations, being respectful to others, managing emotions, and focusing on business while at work. Executives are also expected to support the company, their bosses, their peers, and their employees. While employees might complain about what goes on in an organization or about their bosses, executives are expected to be more discreet about their opinions if it might impact the opinions and/or actions of others. Executives who speak negatively about a company policy or decision that is out of their hands is not doing a service to the company or the people who hear it, and it doesn't reflect well on the executives who speak that way. Executives are expected to support and gain support, or at least adhere to company policies and/or decisions whether or not they agree with them. Assuming the policies are moral, ethical, and legal, executives are expected to carry them out and make sure others do the same.

I had a client who struggled with supporting company decisions that he knew were not going to be well received by his team. Most were human resources policies that were out of his control. He was more comfortable commiserating with his team and blaming the company or human resources department than helping to reinforce these new company policies. His behavior not only hurt the company's ability to carry out the new policies in his division, but also they did not make him look good to his employees, bosses, and the human resources department. His behavior also hurt the morale of his division because he indirectly validated and supported their frustrations rather than helping them accept the policies, implement them, and move on. Executives are expected to support and carry out the policies and decisions of the company.

Executives are expected to refrain from speaking negatively about others including their bosses, peers, and employees—unless it's done appropriately to the right people and it is regarding performance issues. General complaining about others is not considered professional behavior. Executives who complain about their bosses and peers are not only hurting their own perceptions, but also they may hurt the morale of the organization. Complaining about employees is also not becoming. Any performance issues should be addressed appropriately.

Executives are further expected to protect their companies, bosses, and subordinates. They are expected to protect their companies from any potential legal issues, competition, and negative publicity. They are expected to protect their bosses from surprises and bad publicity by keeping them informed and prepared. Executives protect their subordinates and employees from blame and politics at the executives' level and above. Executives are also expected to guide their employees, keep them prepared, and help them avoid making mistakes in public.

Maintaining professionalism during stressful or politically charged situations can be challenging. When fear or anger are triggered, they can overcome our ability to maintain composure and professionalism—significantly hurting our executive presence. Conversely, maintaining composure and professionalism during difficult situations can impress and earn the respect of others. A common scenario that tests executives' abilities to maintain professionalism is when an executive separates from the company— either on the executives' terms or the companies'. If the executives leaving are at all bitter towards their company, this is when it's likely to be seen. No matter what the circumstances are, executives should make every effort to leave gracefully. This means not bad-mouthing the company or any of the people they worked with or for, not complaining about the reasons for the separation, and not having a bad attitude during the transition. Executives who leave gracefully and professionally leave a final, positive lasting impression on the company and those they worked with, regardless of the circumstances. Most executives face a difficult separation at some point in their careers. If or when you do, maintain your professionalism and you'll be able to leave with your head held high, relationships intact, and favorable impressions on the organization.

Influence

I will venture to say that *the* most powerful skill an executive can have is *influence*. Influence, according to Merriam-Webster's Dictionary, is: "the act or power of producing an effect without apparent exertion of force or direct exercise of command." It is the ability to impact the thoughts and decisions of others based on the perceived trust, respect, intelligence, and capabilities earned and seen by others. A great example of this is Benjamin Franklin, who I would argue is one of the most influential people in our American history. He was a very powerful influence during the birth of our country, yet he never held a public office. He had no given authority or title, yet he significantly impacted decisions and changes—all behind the scenes. His opinion was sought after and he was invited to participate.

Influence can be effective at all levels inside and outside of an organization, whether it's influencing workers at the lowest levels of an organization (leading), peers across an organization, leaders at the top, the board, industry media, or even government offices. Think about how powerful an executive could be with influence at all of these levels!

So, how does one develop the ability to influence? It's not easy and it takes time, but it's so important. This is a skill that can take many years to develop. It offers the most growth opportunities for all executives. I'm not referring to the influence achieved easily through money, name, or title. That's almost cheating. I'd be worried about decisions influenced solely by those criteria. I'm talking about influence that's *earned*. Influence is often earned through some combination of these qualities:

- Achieving proven leadership abilities and successes
- Becoming and establishing oneself as an expert in a given field
- Establishing trust and respect
- Demonstrating general well-rounded knowledge to help solve large, complex problems
- Maintaining an objective viewpoint so others know they'll get well-thought-out input and no hidden agendas

- Demonstrating humility so others know the input won't be self-serving or about ego
- Having a network of other respected, influential people

Some individuals have quite a bit of influence but don't know how to use it. Either they don't know how to assert their thoughts and opinions, or they don't have the confidence to do it. If you're one of those people who often get asked their opinion, you may have more influence than you realize. Proactively look for opportunities to participate in problem solving, brainstorming, and decision making to help build upon your influence.

Developing and leveraging influencing skills is an ongoing process and growth opportunity. It can lead to many new and even surprising opportunities. Keep working at it and make the most of your potential while adding value to those you influence.

Authenticity

Another important quality in executives valued by organizations is *authenticity*. Employees want to work for someone who is real, not fake. Being yourself and letting others see who you are builds credibility and trust. Let them see what your interests are, what you're passionate about, and what your beliefs are. Don't be afraid to use your own style, sense of humor (as long as it's appropriate), language, habits (as long as they're not bad habits), and so forth. Let people see the real you.

In this book we discuss leadership skills and behaviors that can be developed. Developing these skills and behaviors won't change who you are as a person—your values, interests, beliefs, background, desires, and so on stay intact. While you're practicing new skills and behaviors, they may feel forced or fake to you because they're new. As long as you believe in what you're doing it will become more comfortable for you the longer you practice it and it will become part of your natural behavior.

A common comment I hear during 360 interviews is the desire for executives to be less formal and relate more to the employees. Some employees want to get to know the executives on a little bit more of a personal level. It's motivating to them to feel like they are working hard for someone they respect, like, and believe in. This does not mean sharing your personal problems at work. I strongly discourage that. You can just share something about your family, hobbies or interests and show interest in employees' families, hobbies and interests. If discussing anything personal is just too uncomfortable for you, striking up informal spontaneous conversations about business can also work. You'll learn more about how the employees think and you'll share with them how you think. Remember, employees consider the key to job satisfaction, employee retention, and motivation is the *boss* they work for.

I'm a big believer in "walking the halls" as a leadership strategy. It helps build relationships and rapport. It provides another opportunity to reinforce the vision and motivate employees. You might meet a high-potential employee who hasn't gotten visibility with you yet. You can learn new things from the front line and keep a beat on the morale of the company. You might learn of new issues that haven't been raised yet or even worse, have been kept from you. You can solicit new ideas. It also gives employees an opportunity to see the real you. It doesn't take a lot of time and the benefits are well worth it. Depending on logistics, management level, and current environment, the amount of time spent walking the halls may differ. I encourage my clients at the senior and executive vice president levels to start by blocking out *at least* thirty minutes a week for walking the halls. Most prefer to do this on Fridays when people are winding down, in good spirits, and social. Every client who has practiced this habit has had great results. They've felt more connected to the employees, learned more about the employees, learned more about the company and what's happening on the front lines, and they have found new risks and opportunities they had not seen before. The results for the employees have been feeling more comfortable with the executives, sharing new ideas they were fearful to bring up in more formal settings, feeling more connected and loyal to the executives, learning leadership practices in real time from the executives through these more casual conversations, and feeling more motivated with these results.

Motivation

All too often I hear executives make comments about how they believe their employees should adjust their working, communication, and motivational needs around the executives' preferred styles. I've heard some say, "They are who they are and their people need to get used to it." Does that sound like someone you'd like to work for? See the section above about humility. One of the key responsibilities of executives is to get the most out of their people in terms of productivity, efforts, and results—in other words, management and *motivation*. In most cases, executives will have many different types of people working for them. This is a good thing. Having a diverse work force offers so many opportunities for new ideas and creative problem solving. This is something to leverage. If you have a team of people who think the same way, work the same way and have the same ideas, you could be missing some great opportunities. But having a diverse team requires more effort in managing them. They will all require different levels of direction, management, motivation, and acknowledgement. Some employees may need a lot of detailed direction. Others might just need to know the expectations and have the freedom to go off and work. Some need more feedback, praise, and acknowledgement to stay motivated. Others might need monetary or promotional rewards. Some want private recognition. Others prefer public acknowledgment. Some need a more personal approach with time to socialize and relate with their bosses. Others just need to know the facts.

Knowing what each employee needs to work at his or her optimum level is the responsibility of the executive. The company, executive, and employee will benefit and grow from this approach. The employee will be motivated and productive. The executive will have a happy, productive team that will help achieve results—and will indirectly and organically make the executive look good. The company will benefit from the high performing teams, results, and low turnover. The bottom line is an effective executive makes the most of his or her team by managing and motivating different people differently to get the best out of each employee.

Role Model

Whether you like it or not—or acknowledge it or not—you are a *role model* for your organization. The employees in your organization look to you to show them what behaviors work, what doesn't work, and what is accepted. They study your behaviors and notice the things you do (or don't do). This is the case for both positive and negative behaviors. Obviously, we'd like to see people in our organizations learn and practice positive behaviors. Unfortunately, they will emulate the negative ones, too. If you arrive late for meetings, you are indirectly sending a message that that is acceptable behavior. If you look at your computer or Blackberry during meetings, you're letting others know that that is acceptable behavior. You can't expect others to "do as I say, not as I do."

While coaching an executive of a technical media organization for one of the largest media companies, I provided eye-opening feedback to him during a 360 Assessment. This particular executive used his Blackberry during all meetings—whether the meeting was with his team, his vendors, or even the CEO of the company. His employees saw this as acceptable behavior because *he* was doing it, so they all started doing the same. When he heard about this behavior being emulated by his employees, it upset him. While he knew it was wrong for him to be using his Blackberry during meetings, he was okay with it and willing to take the risks. When it was brought to his attention that his people were doing the same, he was not okay with that.

This executive also had a relatively tough demeanor in meetings. He came across to others as sarcastic, confrontational, and condescending. Once again, to a certain extent, he was okay with others seeing him that way. But, again, his employees started emulating that behavior—which was not okay. He did not want to see his employees practicing his bad behavior. It was okay for him to take the risks and criticism for these behaviors, but he didn't want his people taking those risks and criticisms. When this executive received this feedback, it really gave him the motivation to change his bad behaviors and be a better role model. When a follow-up 360 was performed later to gauge progress, his peers and employees noted the positive changes they saw in his behavior.

Dress

Over the years, many companies and industries have adopted more casual forms of *dress*. This is not the case with all companies and industries, though. Some executives, after reaching a certain level, believe they've earned the right to dress in whatever way they want, and that may be acceptable. Regardless, as an executive, be thoughtful to the way you dress.

I'm a big believer in dressing for the audience. If it's a casual Friday and you have mostly internal meetings and plan to walk the halls, you may want to dress more casually if that's the culture of the company. If you have formal meetings with external people or organizations (like investors, banks, analysts, and so forth) you might consider dressing more formally. Think about the impression you want to leave with your audience and dress for that. A more formal dress will always make an executive look more commanding. Conversely, a casual dress can make an executive look more creative and entrepreneurial.

There are some executives who believe it doesn't matter how they dress and they dress casually no matter what the circumstances. This is typically seen with executives who have risen through creative or technical environments. This may be acceptable for executives who achieved such a level of success, fame, or notoriety that the way they dress won't have an impact on perception or future success. Good examples include Steve Jobs and Bill Gates. But this is rarely the case. If you have aspirations for more success, then dress the part. When in doubt, overdress!

Summary

<u>Executives</u> grow by developing executive presence because it enhances the perceptions, credibility and reputations of the executives. They earn more respect and will be seen and accepted as leaders because followers will want to follow them—making them more effective.

<u>Companies</u> grow when their executives develop executive presence because it can enhance the reputation of the company. The executives become positive role models for their companies. Leadership effectiveness increases, as does employee morale.

CHAPTER 10:

• •

Networking & Building Relationships

You can make more friends in two months by becoming interested in other people than you can in two years by trying to get other people interested in you.

—Dale Carnegie, How to Win Friends and Influence People

Two skills that pull some executives out of their comfort zones are *networking and building relationships*. Networking is the meeting of individuals for the purpose of exchanging information or services. Networking includes the creating, building, and maintaining of relationships for mutual sharing of information, camaraderie, brainstorming, or just enjoyment. Building relationships is the cultivating and nurturing of relationships so it follows and is an important part of networking. Both are required to build successful, gratifying professional networks. Therefore, through the remainder of this chapter, the term *networking* will be assumed to include building relationships.

Networking provides opportunities for the mutual sharing of

new ideas, helpful (legally appropriate) information or knowledge, or introductions to new people. Networking can be done with old friends, current bosses, colleagues, previous bosses or coworkers, alumni, or any other business acquaintances. Networking also provides more opportunities to build influencing skills.

Executives who don't develop and nurture a network have a narrower base of information, contacts, and sphere of influence. They put themselves in a bit of a bubble, isolated from the world outside their immediate role and company. Not only does this hinder their own exposure and potential opportunities, it also limits the value they bring to their organization by way of information and contacts, too.

Networking provides another source of information. You might speak with or meet with a colleague in your industry to share insights and thoughts on the current state of the marketplace. You might reach out to someone who knows of a potential candidate for an important position you're trying to fill. Perhaps you're looking for a new opportunity for yourself. Networking is the most fruitful method of finding a new job or opportunity. You might learn best practices from your network. Your network can provide sales opportunities. Maybe you're looking for some business or career advice. Your network can be a huge, relevant, and trustworthy source of whatever information you seek. See exhibit 10-a for list of opportunities networking can provide.

Exhibit 10-a Opportunities
Networking Can Provide

- New ideas
- New customers
- New vendors
- New contacts
- Best practices
- Market/Industry knowledge
- Experiences

- Specific expertise
- Political knowledge or contacts
- New technologies
- Candidates
- Job opportunities
- Consultants
- Advice

Unfortunately, many executives wait until they need something, typically a job, to call the people they know and consider part of their network. Doing so can make the call more awkward and uncomfortable. Don't wait until you need something to build or maintain your network. Keep up on it. As you periodically reach out to your contacts, you can learn something you didn't even know to ask about just through normal conversation. You might be able to help them in some way. You also don't want your network to feel used because you only call when you need something.

Networking doesn't work one-way. You have to be willing to be a source for your network, too. By helping others you can help yourself long-term and expand your sphere of influence. You might learn something from the exchange or may need to call on that person to return the favor in the future. Plus, it feels good to help others out.

Building relationships with people you already know externally and internally to your company or enterprise will help you strengthen your network. It's also a great leadership practice internally in your organization and company. Building relationships internally with peers can help you build teamwork and rapport, supports collaboration, enhances creative problem solving and the sharing of information, and provides a positive example for employees. It can also help break down organizational silos. Building relationships down through the organization reinforces open communication, builds teamwork, motivates employees, and provides visibility for yourself and your employees.

So, *how* do you network and build relationships? You can start by coming up with a list of people you've met throughout your career whom you've respected, thought about and wondered how or where they were, or have just wanted to reach out to. Add to your list people in your organization, company, or industry you would like to meet. Spend some concentrated time on this and give it thought. Go through your Rolodex or contact list for people you haven't spoken to in awhile and would like to reconnect with. Prioritize your list and start making calls and plans. You might want to reach out to and talk to some over the phone. You might want to meet others for coffee, breakfast, lunch, or drinks after work.

An executive friend of mine who was uncomfortable networking said that the hardest part for her was making the call to reconnect or just stay in touch. She didn't know what to say. It doesn't have to be complicated or formal. Here is an example: "Hi [their name], it's [your name]. You crossed my mind so I thought I'd reach out and say 'hello'. Let's get together and catch up. When are you available?" The key to keeping conversations flowing in person or on the phone is to ask questions. This helps keep the other person talking, which provides opportunities to learn something new. It also makes the other person feel good because you show interest in them. If you need help with something, wait until later in the conversation. Give yourself and the other individual time to reconnect and get comfortable again. Show the person that you are interested in what's happening with them. If you jump right in asking for help, it can give the impression that your intentions were selfish. Remember, networking is about a *mutual* relationship with people you authentically want to keep in touch with. A nice closing might be: "It was great catching up. I want to make sure we keep in touch so let's do this again." Then put a reminder in your calendar for an appropriate lapse of time to schedule another get-together. In some cases you might follow up with an email thanking the other person for joining you and reiterating your desire to keep in touch.

If you don't know the people you want to meet personally, use your network to find someone to make the introduction. LinkedIn provides a fantastic avenue for networking. You can reconnect with old colleagues and link to new contacts that way.

Building relationships internally can occur the same way—through phone calls, coffee, breakfasts, lunches, golf, drinks, dinner, or other events. Walking the halls and engaging in informal conversations is also a great way to build relationships. Just like networking, it takes conscious effort and planning but it's worth the investment.

There are many places to meet new people and build a professional network aside from your organization. Some options include conferences and conventions, industry associations, and community service opportunities. Many are uncomfortable meeting new people because they don't know how to start the conversation. When you've identified someone you would like to meet, think of a safe, open-ended question relevant to the event or industry. Some examples include: "What did you think of that presentation (or speaker)?"; "How far did you travel for this event?"; "What do you do for [company name]?"; or "How long have you worked with [company name]?". Once you have a question prepared in your mind, introduce yourself and ask it. Remember, the key to keeping conversations going is to ask questions. Let your natural curiosity take part.

Networking and building relationships is an ongoing process. You've hopefully developed a good list of people to start with for making calls and plans, and a list of events where you can meet new people. Use your new time management tool and plan for the time you will devote to networking on a periodic basis—whether it's weekly, monthly, or quarterly. Schedule time for reviewing your contacts to create your list of people to reconnect with and plan for the meetings. Keep up on it and it can provide a valuable source of information, as well as enjoyable relationships—and even lasting friendships.

Summary

Executives grow through networking and building relationships because those activities expand their breadth of knowledge and resources as well as their sphere of influence.

Companies grow when executives network and build relationships because the executives can gather more information and ideas, and make connections on behalf of the company—whether it's with new customers or vendors, or other influential people. Internally it promotes teamwork and the sharing of information.

CHAPTER 11:

● ●

The Numbers

People with low financial literacy standards are often unable to take their ideas and create assets out of them.

—*Robert Kiyosaki*

Whether you are a manager, executive, or business owner, you need to understand the *numbers*. You need to understand how decisions impact the bottom line. Even if you're an executive of a creative organization, it will be in your best interest as well as in the interest of your company for you to understand financial data. If you don't currently have responsibilities for revenue, expenses, or profit, you will at some point. This doesn't mean you need to understand the details of accounting, how to use Excel, or have the training of a financial analyst. You need to understand the basics of how financial statements work and the general properties of each account. You also need to understand the assumptions that go into your long-term plans, yearly budgets, and current forecasts. Finally, you need to have an understanding of the metrics used to gauge performance.

Wait! Don't skip this chapter! I know some of you are rolling your eyes hoping and praying you'll never have to deal with *financials*.

Some of you are having panic attacks at the thought of it. I know it seems daunting and scary. It doesn't have to be. Take a deep breath and we'll go through how to get comfortable with it. First, keep in mind that most numbers-driven reports—whether financial reports or metrics—are based on just two pieces of information: the numbers and the assumptions used to determine those numbers. Financial calculations in most financial statements or other data-driven reports are nothing more than basic math—addition, subtraction, multiplication, and division. You're not going to have to do it in your head. There seems to be a fear among many executives that we'll be expected to do calculations on the fly in our heads. This isn't an old math class. Computers and calculators are acceptable. In fact, as a prior financial executive, I admit I became so reliant on calculators that I once caught myself adding $100 plus $100 on a calculator. Don't sweat it if you're not good at doing math in your head. Secondly, it's more important that you understand the reasons for the numbers, what's included in the numbers, and what assumptions were used to create the numbers. If numbers themselves make you nervous, focus more on their meaning.

I have seen careers soar because an executive understood the basics of the numbers and therefore understood the impact decisions have on them; they also knew what questions to ask that uncovered potential issues or even opportunities. Conversely, I have seen executives get held back in their careers or even fired from positions because of decisions made without an understanding of the financial implications. Keeping your head in the sand about the numbers can be a risky position to take and can hold you back from finding potentially new opportunities.

Financial Statements are made up of basically three statements – the Income Statement (or Profit & Loss Statement, or P&L), the Balance Sheet, and the Cash Flow Statement. In addition to knowing the basics of each, you also need to know how they interrelate.

The income statement reflects the profit (or loss) for each period. It's basically revenue minus expenses. The difference between revenue and sales is revenue can include any income earned that is not from the sale of goods or services. Examples include royalties, licenses, and interest. You need to understand how revenue is calculated and reported. For example, is the cash or accrual method used? The cash method means revenue and expenses are reported when the cash is received or paid. The accrual method accounts for revenue and expenses when they happen, regardless of when the cash is received or spent. You also need to understand the components of the expenses. What are the largest, what are the most volatile, which ones are fixed, and which ones can be controlled? Don't ignore the small expenses either. Many times good savings can be found in lots of little numbers.

In some cases your income statement may include *gross profit,* which is revenue minus direct expenses (Costs of Goods Sold or COGS) or those expenses incurred on labor or materials used directly on the product or service. General and Administrative (G&A) expenses are overhead. These are expenses for the infrastructure of the business, not the product or service itself. Many times G&A expenses offer the most opportunity and scrutiny for cost reductions. Net income is profit or revenue minus *all* expenses. A common acronym (and term) used in financial statements is EBITDA, which stands for *earnings before interest, taxes, depreciation, and amortization.* EBITDA is used to measure the operational profitability of a company by removing non-cash (depreciation and amortization) and non-operational (taxes) items. See exhibit 11-a for the basic structure of a P&L.

Exhibit 11-a: Basic Structure of a P&L Statement

<u>Sales</u>

<u>- COGS</u>

<u>= Gross Margin</u>

<u>- G&A</u>

<u>= EBITDA</u>

<u>+/- Interest, Taxes,</u>

<u>Depreciation, Amortization</u>

<u>= Net Income</u>

The balance sheet balances assets (what the company owns, such as buildings, equipment, cars, and so on) versus liabilities (what the company owes including loans) and stockholders' equity (ownership in the company). Hence the basic balance sheet rule is Assets = Liabilities + Stockholders Equity. Learn what's included in your assets and liabilities and how decisions impact them.

Both the income statement and balance sheet have non-cash items. These are items that impact those statements but are numbers "on paper" only that may not impact cash. Examples include depreciation and amortization.

The purpose of depreciation and amortization is to match revenue and expenses over time. There can be large expenditures paid or revenue received in one year that impact more than just that year. For example, a large piece of equipment may be purchased one year that generates product to be sold over many years. Depreciation allows for the matching of this expenditure with the revenue received over time. This is helpful in two ways. First, it helps prevent significantly fluctuating P&L's or large losses in one year, because these typically large expenditures aren't reflected in just the year of purchase. Secondly, there are tax implications. Since depreciation is a pretax item, it reduces the amount of income used to calculate taxes each year. Depreciation impacts P&L's as well as Balance Sheets because the yearly deprecation amount is added to the P&L as an expense and the same amount is deducted from the asset on the Balance Sheet as the asset loses value over time.

Amortization is similar to depreciation but spreads out large amounts of revenue over time. Large amounts of revenue can also be received in one year but the associated expenses may occur over time. Amortization allows for the spreading of revenue over the time the expenses occur. Examples include multi-year contracts a company may be partially paid for upfront but has to deliver the products or services over more than one year. The term *amortization* is also used for the pay down of the principle of a loan, or the spreading out of intangible assets (intellectual property) over time. The important thing to remember is what the purpose of depreciation and amortization is and how it impacts the P&L, Balance Sheet, and taxes.

The Cash Flow Statement helps reconcile the non-cash items with the cash items so there's a clear understanding of the cash position. I have worked in large corporations where cash was managed at the corporate level, so little attention was spent on cash flow. Conversely, smaller companies have a tendency to focus only on cash and ignore the income statement. Business owners assume that if they have enough cash in the bank they're profitable, right? Then they are surprised when the income statement says something different. Almost every decision made will have some impact on a financial statement whether it impacts revenue, expenses, assets, liabilities, or cash. That's why it's so important to understand how the statements work and what they say.

Financial statements are used in many ways. They help gauge the health of a company, calculate taxes, and report performance. They're used internally to make decisions and externally to help get loans, determine the worth for potential acquisition or mergers, and they are sometimes benchmarked against other companies for comparisons. If it's a public company, the financial statements tell the world and investment community how the company is doing.

In addition to financial statements, there are some calculations and ratios often used to gauge performance or make decisions; these can also cause some angst among non-finance executives. The most common ones are summarized in exhibit 11-b. With the exception of ROI and Break-Even (which can be calculated by your finance representative, accountant, or with online calculators) most ratios are simple calculations with numbers that can be found on the financial statements. *What is more important is that you know what they mean and what they are used for.*

Karen Lindsey

Exhibit 11-b: Commonly Used Financial Calculations and Ratios		
<u>Calculation or Ratio</u>	<u>Formula</u>	<u>Purpose</u>
Gross Profit	Revenue – Cost of Goods Sold	Depicts profit from direct materials and labor used for generating revenue. Used to manage revenue and direct expenses.
Gross Profit Margin	Gross Profit ÷ Revenue	Provides profit as a percent of revenue. Used to gauge revenue, operational efficiencies, and costs
Net Income	Revenue – All Expenses	Provides total profit. Considered the *bottom line.*
Net Profit Margin	Net Income ÷ Revenue	Provides total profit as a percent of revenue. Used to gauge total company performance.
ROI (Return on Investment)	Investment Profit* ÷ Cost of Investment	Indicates potential money to be made or lost on an investment. Used to make decisions on investments.
Break-even Point	Revenue = Variable Expenses + Fixed Expenses	Point at which sales (in units or dollars) cover the costs of an investment; total revenue equals total expenses.
Working Capital	Current Assets – Current Liabilities	Illustrates amount of liquid assets available for operational use. Used to gauge cash flow risks and operational health.
Accounts Receivable Turnover Ratio	Revenue ÷ Average Accounts Receivable**	Gauges efficiencies in managing accounts receivable. A high ratio implies efficient collection of receivables.

Exhibit 11-b: Commonly Used Financial Calculations and Ratios		
Calculation or Ratio	Formula	Purpose
Inventory Turnover	Sales ÷ Inventory	Illustrates number of times inventory is sold and replaced over a period of time. Low ratio may indicate poor sales and excess inventory. High ratio could indicate stock shortage risk.
Debt to Equity Ratio	Total Liabilities ÷ Total Stockholder's Equity	Measures financial leverage of a company. A high debt ratio means the company has financed operations with more debt than equity and could indicate cash flow risks. A low ratio could indicate opportunities to finance revenue growth.
Earnings Per Share (EPS)	Net Income ÷ Number of Common Shares Outstanding	Illustrates amount of earnings for each outstanding share. Indicates a company's profitability. Used to determine the price of shares.
PE Ratio (Price Earnings Ratio)	Market Price of Common Stock Per Share ÷ Earnings Per Share	Measures price per share relative to earnings per share. Used to determine value of shares. A high ratio indicates a high price for the earnings, or a more expensive investment.

* A more accurate ROI requires a more complicated calculation using the time value of money. Easy-to-use calculators can be found online or in Excel.

**Average Accounts Receivable = (Beginning Accounts Receivable – Ending Accounts Receivable)/2

Long-term plans, budgets, and forecasts are used to plan ahead and measure performance. Long-term plans span over several years, typically three to five. Other terms used for long-term plans include long-range plans, strategic plans, five-year plans, and three-year plans. Long-term plans help an organization think about and plan for the future. Organizations should think about how the market, competition, technology, regulations, politics, and any other situations may impact them and their financial position over time. Long-term plans can help an organization prepare for future new projects, new product offerings, and new investments.

Budgets are used to plan for, provide guidance for and monitor the financial progress of an organization in a fiscal year. Another term for budgets is "operating plans." Budgets are prepared before the start of a new fiscal year and project how revenue and expenses are expected to be realized for that year. Actual results from financial statements are compared against the budget throughout the year to determine any financial issues or opportunities that may arise.

Forecasts are updated projections for the current year. Things can change so quickly and often that budgets can become obsolete after the first month of the fiscal year. Forecasts are basically updated budgets that account for these changes. Forecasts incorporate the actual financial results realized and reported to date (called actuals) with projections for the remainder of the year. For example, a May forecast will include actuals through the end of April and updated projections for the rest of the fiscal year.

The most important part of Long-term plans, budgets, and forecasts are the *assumptions* used to estimate each number contained within. Since each of these financial tools is projecting the future—and there aren't any reliable crystal balls yet—assumptions are used to generate the numbers. These assumptions are critical to the validity of the projections and each of these tools is only as good as the assumptions used. Assumptions may be based on: past information with adjustments for changes, anticipated decisions about people, products, projects, customers, purchases, and so forth. Assumptions might also be based on numbers plugged in as placeholders due to the lack of information.

It's all of these assumptions that I encourage executives to pay attention to and ask questions about. The assumptions contain information that can be the indicators of risks and opportunities. Understanding these assumptions will help executives have a better grasp of their financial projections.

Actual financial results are often compared to the original budget, forecast, and prior year results over the course of the year (typically monthly or quarterly) to gauge performance and identify risks or opportunities. I encourage executives to review financial results monthly to allow for enough time to make decisions or course corrections quickly and as needed. Forecasts are also often compared to budget to see what has changed and what the trends are. When reviewing these financial reports, please be aware of which comparisons are favorable and unfavorable. Financial reports can be confusing based on how the favorable and unfavorable numbers are presented. For example, a negative number may just be the result of subtracting one number from another but it may reflect a positive outcome. If expenses went down compared to the forecast or prior year, the number may be negative but the result is positive—expenses went down. Parentheses can also be used to report results. Just make sure you know what those results mean.

Internally, *metrics* are also used to gauge operational performance. Metrics are data that provide comparisons, trends, or projections; they are often unique to industries and sometimes to companies and departments based on the type of operations and key drivers of the business. Metrics may be based on labor hours, product outputs, time, sales, expenses, or any combination of these. Metrics allow a company to track and measure performance against the past, other companies, other departments, or industry standards. You need to understand the key metrics used in your organization and company, and how they are calculated so you understand what and how decisions impact the results.

There are many opportunities to learn about your financial statements and metrics. You can start with your accounting or finance departments. Schedule a meeting and ask them to explain each to you. Have a copy of the financial statements or metrics in front of you and ask questions about each line. If you're in a smaller company and don't have accounting or finance departments, consult with your accountant. There are books available as well as classes about finance for non-finance people. Don't be afraid to ask for help. Once you get over the fear and gain a basic understanding of the numbers that impact your organization, company and industry, it will make your job easier and reduce the risk of making decisions without understanding the financial implications. By the way, it will also help alleviate your anxiety about the numbers. As an executive or business owner, having a basic understanding of the numbers will help you know what questions to ask and may uncover potential issues or opportunities you may otherwise not be aware of.

If you're already a successful business owner or executive and are embarrassed to ask questions about the numbers, do it now, before an uncomfortable and/or public situation arises that shows your lack of understanding. It will only get worse if you wait. Get that knowledge under your belt and it will reduce your risks, offer opportunities, and give you more confidence in your decisions.

Summary

<u>Executives</u> grow by knowing and understanding the numbers and financial measurements because it enhances their ability to make informed decisions as well as find new important decisions to be made. Issues can be identified more proactively and new opportunities can be found.

<u>Companies</u> grow when executives know and understand the numbers because more informed decisions will be made, profit and productivity will be maximized, and more company risks and opportunities can be proactively identified.

CHAPTER 12:

• •

Managing Your Career

Think not of yourself as the architect of your career but as the sculptor. Expect to have to do a lot of hard hammering and chiseling and scraping and polishing.

—*BC Forbes*

Throughout this book we've explored the leadership skills necessary to maximize the growth of our careers and our organizations. We have to proactively manage our growth and our careers. We cannot expect our bosses, companies, mentors, human resources departments, or anyone else to manage our development or careers for us. Others certainly have input, feedback, and influence over them. Some even have some control (temporarily) over our current jobs and career paths, but we are ultimately responsible for making our own decisions and managing our careers.

Managing our careers should not be a passive response to where our jobs, skills and opportunities take us. Proactive thought, planning, and action should constantly be taken to guide us where we want to go. Circumstances and opportunities may change our direction, but we should never relinquish control or let others decide for us our career paths.

Most of us start our careers in a tactical role with skills we learned from college or from our first few jobs. Then the higher we climb in the management structure the more leadership skills are required to be successful. Most of these leadership skills are not taught in school or even in our jobs. We learn them from watching others, from guidance we receive from others, and from training classes we sign up for. In some cases we might not even be aware of the skills we are lacking or haven't fully developed that could be holding us back. Most of these leadership skills are needed no matter what direction we go or which ladder we climb. That's why it's so important to take stock of the skills that are our strengths to leverage and those that need more development, so we can do what we need to do to set ourselves up for success.

We may not always be aware of the skills that others perceive as our strengths or weaknesses. These might be blind spots for us. That's why feedback is so valuable. Whenever possible and appropriate, seek and embrace feedback from your bosses, peers, mentors, direct reports, customers, and anyone else appropriate to ask. I think everyone should have at least one 360 Assessment done at some point in his or her career to gain insights into the perceptions others have of our strengths and growth opportunities and how they differ from our own. The ideal scenario is to have three 360 Assessments done throughout a career, one at each level of management. A first assessment would occur during the first or second management position after some experience has been gained; a second would occur while being in middle management; and another at executive levels. If having three is not possible, having one at middle management would be the next best option. At that point, a lot of experience has been gained yet there's a lot of time to take advantage of the feedback and any changes made. Regardless, it's never too late to have one done and the outcome can be career and life changing.

There are basically two ways we can grow as individuals—in our skills and in our experiences. Both should be carefully considered when mapping our career paths. Through feedback, advice from bosses and mentors, and our own research, we can gain an understanding of where we need to grow in our skills and experiences so we can seek opportunities to develop them.

Once we know what skills we need and want to develop, we need a plan to do it. Developing specific skills doesn't just happen; it requires opportunity and effort. We can develop our skills by taking advantage of leadership development programs, books, classes, seminars, advanced degrees, leadership associations, coaching, and even through concentrated efforts on specific skills. Create an actionable plan for how you're going to develop your skills, and follow through seeking feedback along the way to ensure progress is being made and seen. Exhibit 12-a is an example of a growth plan for specific skills.

Exhibit 12-a: Growth Plan	
Develop Strategic Thinking Skills	
1) Review the *Wall Street Journal*	Daily (8:00 – 8:30 a.m.)
2) Read industry trade publication	Monthly
3) Add strategic questions to weekly meetings with direct reports	Immediately, ongoing
4) Find two strategic thinkers and schedule time with them	By end of month
5) Plan a meeting to brainstorm strategic challenges and opportunities; determine the research and reading required prior to the meeting; find a facilitator	By end of month
Build & Leverage Professional Network	
1) Create list of existing contacts to reach out to	By end of week

Exhibit 12-a: Growth Plan	
2) Make calls to existing contacts list and schedule breakfasts and lunches	By end of month
3) Create list of desired new contacts (by name or position)	By end of next week
4) Make calls to new contacts and schedule breakfasts and lunches	By end of next month
5) Find two industry meetings or conventions to attend and make plans to go	By end of month
6) Attend the two industry meetings or conventions	By end of year
7) Find two more industry networking opportunities and make plans to attend	By end of next month
8) Find and join a leadership association	By end of next month
9) Create new list of existing contacts to reach out to, make calls, and schedule meetings	Quarterly
10) Create new list of desired contacts, make calls, and schedule meetings	Bi-annually

New and different experiences provide growth through the learning opportunities and skills developed under different circumstances, in different roles, and in different environments. There are many ways of seeking new experiences for growth opportunities. First, think about the experiences that will help you achieve the growth you're looking for. If it's early in your career or if you're in middle management, you might need more management experience, opportunities to manage other managers, cross-functional project experience, strategic experience, operational experience, and so forth. Often, you can find opportunities in your current role and company by asking for it or volunteering for special projects or cross-functional projects. You can also volunteer to take on the tough company challenges, or take a risk and create a project on your own that addresses some significant business challenges or opportunities.

If you can't find opportunities for personal growth in your current role, look into new roles in your current company. If you can't find the growth opportunities in your current company, consider finding a new company. Remember, you're responsible for your own growth. If your boss or company can't provide it for you, consider other options.

Those already in executive roles might need to gain experiences managing a full P&L (or stand alone business), working internationally, managing large-scale projects, working in a corporate role versus business unit (line role) or vice versa, doing public speaking, doing mergers and acquisitions, or reporting to a board. You might be able to gain some of these experiences in your existing role with new projects or expanded responsibilities. Others might require a job change within or outside of your company. Executives shouldn't shy away from taking risks and taking on the tough challenges. Valuable experiences and personal growth can be gained that can lead to new opportunities.

In general, changing jobs and changing companies can provide growth and motivation with new experiences and opportunities, new challenges, new cultures, exposure to different management styles, and so on. Staying in one role at one company for a long period of time can limit the growth opportunities available. Think about the differences in experience gained being in one job for six years or three different jobs over six years. Be proactive about the experiences you need and want for your growth and go get them.

Some people have a tendency to fear success. They see what their bosses do and wonder if they're capable of ever being able to do it. Some don't feel worthy of the titles. Don't limit your own success, especially when others see the potential in you to go further. Identify and work on the areas you feel insecure about and challenge yourself. Many executives feel overwhelmed and in over their heads when they initially take on new roles. They learn and grow into them. Give yourself the opportunity to do the same.

Conversely, some people follow a career path without thought to whether or not it's what they really want. They may have chosen a specific career because they were influenced by others or following in someone else's footsteps. Some realize later they don't enjoy their fields of work. Some don't like the responsibilities associated with different levels of management. As we consider our individual career paths and what the requirements are at each level of management, it's important to take stock of what we want out of our jobs and careers, and how well our chosen path will provide it.

We also have to manage our expectations about our capabilities and willingness to do what is required of a role. Some of us blindly follow a path pushing for higher levels and more responsibilities because we feel we're supposed to rather than deciding if it's what we really want and something we're capable of doing. For example, some climb the ladder and reach a role that requires too much travel or not enough work/life balance and decide to take steps back to get the balance they need. Some expect bigger titles because they have seniority and not necessarily because they have the skills. As you think about your path, consider the day-to-day activities, levels of responsibilities, work/life balance, travel requirements, and anything else that's important to you; and balance your expectations of the jobs with your skills and experience. Be true to yourself to find the career path that's right for you.

Summary

Executives grow by developing skills and gaining new experiences that can then lead to opportunities for developing new skills and gaining even more experiences. Executives can maximize their potential and play at the top of their game. The search for growth should be never-ending.

Companies grow when their executives grow because the companies receive the benefit of the growth in skills and broad experiences. Even if employees leave to pursue their own growth, companies will avoid dealing with unhappy, unmotivated or potentially risk-adverse employees, and will benefit from new perspectives and experiences from the new employees taking their place. Companies with highly effective leaders experience higher productivity, a more motivated and happy workforce, well-managed risks, and the ability to develop new opportunities for company growth.

ABOUT THE AUTHOR

· ·

Karen is a renowned executive coach and leadership development consultant. She has worked with mid and senior level executives from The Walt Disney Company, ESPN, Comcast, HBO, NBCUniversal, MTVN, FremantleMedia, Fox, Warner Bros., Alliance Bernstein, Cushman & Wakefield, and others.

In additional to executive coaching, Karen conducts leadership training programs, seminars, and meeting facilitations. Topics have included leadership skills, communication, project management, team building, motivation, operational planning, financial modeling, and others.

Prior to executive coaching, Karen spent twenty years in the global entertainment, design, production, construction, manufacturing, online, and consumer products industries for such companies as The Walt Disney Company, Warner Bros., and ESPN.

Karen has a BS in Finance and an MBA in Management & Organizational Behavior. She is also a certified Organizational & Executive Coach from New York University.

Karen has been a contributor on Fox Television for business and career topics and has been featured on variety.com and WDRC Radio.

INDEX

• •

155

P

Participants 3, 12, 72, 75–76, 80, 82, 86, 96–101

Participation 10–11, 13, 51, 73, 74, 100, 115

Past 4, 6, 42, 50, 60, 64–65, 140–141

PDA 21, 24

Peer pressure 15

Peers 3, 64–66, 72–74, 102, 113, 116–119, 124, 129, 146

Perceive 71, 146

Perception 1, 8, 67, 71, 82, 84, 110, 115, 117, 124–125, 146

Perform 62, 67

Performance 14, 37, 57, 59–67, 111, 117–118, 133, 137–138, 140–141

Performance reviews 59, 62–65, 66

Personal ix, 14, 24, 41, 88, 97, 114–116, 121–122, 149

Personalities 8, 54, 108

Peter Drucker 17

Philip Armour 53

Philosophies 1, 50

Plan 11–14, 20–23, 26–28, 32, 34–35, 40, 51–52, 67, 90, 92, 96, 98, 124, 129, 131, 133, 140, 147–148

Planning 11, 14, 26, 28, 36, 40, 62, 130, 145, 153

Plateau ix

Position 2, 40, 54–57, 67–70, 85, 113, 128, 134, 137, 140, 146, 148

Positive x, 15, 51, 64–67, 96, 118, 123–125, 129, 141

Potential ix–x, 16, 34, 44, 47, 50, 53, 55, 66, 82, 88, 103, 111, 118, 120–121, 128, 134, 137–138, 142, 149–150

Power 4, 29, 33, 75, 115, 119

Powerful 4, 59, 64, 72–73, 75, 77, 86, 107, 113–114, 119

Power of Habit 29

Practice iii, x, 16, 45, 48, 51, 64–66, 80–81, 86, 98, 103, 108, 120–121, 123, 128–129

Practices iii, 45, 48, 51, 121, 128

Pratt & Whitney 2

Price Earnings Ratio (PE Ratio) 139

Priorities ix, 26–28, 31–33, 37, 43, 44, 49, 51, 62, 102, 112

Proactive 145, 149

Procedures 12

Process 3–4, 6, 11, 18, 20, 22–26, 32, 34–35, 40, 49–51, 54–57, 62, 67, 70, 74–76, 80–81, 95, 112, 120, 131

Productive 7, 9, 31, 86, 88, 92–93, 97, 99, 103–105, 122

Productivity 18, 37, 53–54, 59, 70, 95, 100, 122, 143, 151

Professional ix–x, 55, 107, 111, 116–117, 127, 130, 147

Professional growth ix–x

Profit 3, 61, 133–135, 138, 143

Profit & Loss Statement (P & L) 134

Programs ix, 147, 153

Progress 7, 14–15, 26, 41, 44, 59, 67, 101, 104, 124, 140, 147

Project 9–13, 18–20, 22–24, 32, 35–37, 39, 41–45, 48–51, 60, 62, 72–73, 101, 108, 112, 140, 148–149, 153

Project management principles 10

Promote 4, 10, 69–70, 73, 75, 77, 87, 97, 108–109, 132

Psychological 19

W

Edwards Brothers Malloy
Oxnard, CA USA
October 29, 2013